THE LAST MESSAGE

*In the Name of Allah,
the Compassionate, the Merciful*

THE LAST MESSAGE

The Institute for Compilation and Publication
of Imam Khomeini's Works
(International Affairs Department)

The Last Message

Publisher: The Institute for Compilation and Publication of Imam Khomeini's Works (International Affairs Department)

Translator: A Group of Translators

First Printing:

Copies: 3000

Price: 15000 Rls.

Address: No. 5 Sudeh Alley, Yaser Street, Bahonar Avenue, Jamaran, P.C. 19778, P.O. Box 19575/614, Tehran, Islamic Republic of Iran

Tel: (0098-21) 22283138, 22290191-5

Fax: (0098-21) 22290478

E-mail: international-dept@imam-Khomeini.ir

وصیتنامه امام خمینی به زبان انگلیسی

TABLE OF CONTENTS

Summary and Explanation i
Childhood ii
Period of Studying and Teaching ii
Period of Struggle and Uprising iii
Period in Exile v
Culmination and Victory of the Islamic Revolution………..................... vi
Formation of the Islamic Government and Its Outcome ix
Demise of the Supreme Leader of the Islamic Revolution xv
Children and Family xvi
Literary Works and Compilations xix
Imam Khomeini's Last Will and Testament ………………………….....1
First Supplement to the Last Will and Testament 79
Second Supplement to the Last Will and Testament 89

In the name of God, the Compassionate, the Merciful

A Summary of the Life and Struggles of Imam Khomeini (pbuh)

Familiarizing oneself with the particular circumstances and different aspects of the life of Imam Khomeini (pbuh), a personality who led the greatest revolution in contemporary history, will always prove to be interesting and instructive for those residing outside of Iran. The environment into which he was born; how he was raised; who his teachers and lecturers were; when he married and started a family and under what circumstances; and eventually how he managed to seize the most important strategic Western base in the Middle East region despite the power and undeniable dominance of America over Iran and in the face of the support given the governing regime in that country at the time by the powerful governments, are topics worthy of discussion and deliberation and from which one can derive guidance.

In addition, the issues surrounding the victory of the Islamic Revolution in Iran will prove to be even more interesting and instructive to a researcher, politician, sociologist, and the such like. Why weren't the politicians, the thinkers and the military men, who were connected to and dependent on America and were controlling all the country's organs, successful in preserving the two-thousand-five-hundred-year-old monarchical regime despite the extensive efforts made by America in this regard? And why was all that systematic investment by Western governments in Iran, the spread of debauchery and corruption amongst the young people, the encouragement of a spirit of apathy and indifference amongst various segments of society--all of which stemmed from the most up-to-date investigations--futile? Why couldn't the espionage organizations and the intelligence networks, who have the best people and experts in their employ to administer their affairs and who spend mind-boggling amounts of money on expanding their networks, play a preventative role and stop the Islamic Revolution from occurring? To what extent were the propaganda machines and the mass media of the world's imperious governments--having behind them the experience of decades of rumormongering and spreading disinformation and possessing the magical power to change realities and distort the truth--effective in stopping the progressive waves of the Islamic Revolution? And finally could the Islamic revolution in Iran, with the certain uniqeness that it has, be repeated in other Muslim countries of the world and could it become a suitable role model for all oppressed countries of the third world still under the yoke of colonialism? All these are matters worthy of deliberation and investigation, not only by foreigners, but also by anyone who is a believer and thinker and who worries about the political and cultural situation of his society.

Certainly expanding on all of these topics, even briefly, is not possible in this introduction. However, the most salient points and important events of the life of that great man can be commented on and divided into the following headings:

a) Childhood;
b) Period of Studying and Teaching;
c) Period of Struggle and Uprising
d) Period in Exile;
e) Culmination and Victory of the Islamic Revolution;
f) Formation of the Islamic Government and Its Outcome;
g) The Demise of the Supreme Leader of the Islamic Revolution;
h) Children and the Family;
i) Literary Works and Compilations of Imam Khomeini (pbuh).

a) Childhood

Imam Ruhullah al-Musawi al-Khomeini was born on September 24, 1902 (Shahrivar 30, 1281 AHS/1320 AS) into a family of strong religious traditions in Khomein, a small town some 349 kilometers to the southwest of Tehran. On February 9, 1903 (Bahman 20, 1281 AHS/Dhul-Qadah 11, 1320 AS), just a few months after his birth, his father, Ayatullah Seyyed Mustafa Musawi, was martyred by agents of some rich landowners (Khans) supported by the government of the time, as a consequence of having championed the cause of some of their tenant farmers. Thus, from childhood, Imam Khomeini was acquainted with the pain of not having a father and with the meaning of martyrdom.

His childhood and youth were spent under the care of his devout mother, Banu Hajar, herself from a family of piety and learning, and his respected aunt, Sahebeh Khanom, a brave and militant lady. At the age of fifteen, however, he lost both mother and aunt in the course of a single year.

b) Period of Studying and Teaching

Until the age of nineteen, His Holiness Imam Khomeini remained in Khomein where he received his elementary education from the teachers in that town. The subjects he studied included Arabic literature, logic, dogmatic theology and Islamic jurisprudence. In 1921 (1299 AHS/1339 AS) he went to study religious science in Arak at a theology institute there, and a year later he moved to the city of Qom to continue his studies. There, in addition to completing his previous studies with the religious experts (fuqaha) and religious authorities (mujtahedin) of the time, he also learned mathematics, astronomy and philosophy. It was here that he attended lectures on ethics and Islamic mysticism and for a period of six years he studied the most advanced levels of applied and theoretical mysticism under the late Ayatullah Aqamirza Muhammad-Ali Shahabadi.

Imam's period of teaching began in 1929 (1307 AHS/1347 AS), when he was 27 years old, with lectures in Islamic philosophy, and throughout the rest of his stay in Qom, the subjects he taught there were Islamic philosophy, theoretical mysticism, jurisprudence, the principles of jurisprudence and Islamic ethics.

c) Period of Struggle and Uprising

Based on existing documents, Imam's struggle began in the early years of his adolesence and continued throughout the period of study in various forms against social corruption and ideological and moral deviations. In 1941 (1322 AHS), in what is considered to be his first public political statement, Imam wrote and published a book entitled kashfol-asrarin which he revealed the crimes of the 20 years monarchy of Reza Shah. The book is essentially a detailed, systematic critique of an anti-religious tract, and in defending Islam and spirituality, Imam refutes the deviatory sophisms employed by the author. It is in this book that the idea of an Islamic government, and the need for an uprising to establish this, is propounded.

Imam's overt struggle against Muhammad Reza's regime began in 1960 (1341 AHS) with his opposition to the Provincial and District Council Bill which essentially sought eradication of Islam. With its approval by the government of the time, the Islamic stipulations concerning voters and candidates were dropped and the pledge of all allegiance was changed from swearing "on the Holy Quran" to swearing "on the Holy Book". Imam rose up in opposition to the bill and invited the other maraje, the theological schools and the people to rise up with him.

Following Imam's warnings to the government in the form of telegrams to the prime minister of the time, along with his revelatory speeches and trenchant declarations and coupled with the support given by the maraje as well as the widespread demonstration of the people in Qom, Tehran and other cities, the Shah's regime was forced to retreat from its stands and rescind the bill. The struggle continued, and the regime, in a precipitous move on March 22, 1963 (Farvardin 2, 1342 AHS) attacked the Feyziyeh theological center in Qom. Imam's messages and the speeches on this tragic incident were distributed throughout Iran, and on the afternoon of ashura 1383 AS (June 3, 1963/Khordad 13, 1342 AHS), in a hard-hitting speech, he revealed the secret relations, the agreements and the friendship existing between the Shah and Israel. Subsequently, at 3 am in the morning of June 5 (Khordad 15), Imam's home was surrounded by commandos and as dawn broke, the Leader of the Revolution was arrested and taken to Tehran.

The response of the people was immediate. As news of Imam's arrest broke around the country, the people took to the streets in the early hours of June 5 and staged protest demonstrations. The largest of these took place in the city of Qom, and as soldiers intervened, large numbers of people were martyred. With the announcement of martial law in Tehran, the suppression of the people's demonstrations on that and the following day reached new heights with the resultant deaths of thousands of innocent people.

The tragedy of June 5 was so great that news of it spread across the borders. The pressure of public opinion and the protests of the ulema and people from different areas within the country and outside it eventually forced the regime to free Imam after a ten-month period of imprisonment and house arrest.

Imam's struggle continued with the delivery of revelatory speeches and the publication of disclosing messages. The approval of the "Capitulation Bill" by the government of the time, according to which American political and military advisers would receive judicial immunity, angered the Leader of the Revolution. As soon as he was informed of this treachery, he began a widespread struggle against the bill. He sent messengers to different areas of Iran to inform the people of his decision to deliver a speech on October 26, 1964 (Aban 4, 1341 AHS/Jamadiyolthani 20, 1383 AS) revealing the regime's plans. Despite the serious threat issued by the regime concerning his proposed speech against the Capitulation Bill, Imam delivered what was to become one of the most famous of his speeches on the day he had planned to do so, and in it he severely reproved and humiliated the American president and government.

The Shah's regime saw the solution to their problem to lie in the expulsion of Imam. At dawn on November 4, 1964 (Aban 13, 1343 AHS), Imam's home was once again surrounded by hundreds of commandos and paratroopers. Imam was arrested by the regime's agents and taken straight to Mehrabad Airport in Tehran from where, according to previously arranged agreement, he was sent first to Ankara and then into exile in Bursa, a city in the west of Turkey. There, under the observation of the security forces of the two countries, he was forbidden from carrying out any form of social or political activity.

d) Period in Exile

Imam's stay in Turkey lasted for eleven months and during this time, the Shah's regime, through the use of unprecedented draconian measures, broke what remained of the resistance in Iran. Imam's compulsory stay in Turkey, gave him an invaluable opportunity to compile his great work Tahrirol-Wasila. In this book, which is in fact his practical treatise (resalah), for the first time in that period, opinions governing holy war (jihad), defense, enjoining good and forbidding that which is wrong, and current problems were presented.

On October 5, 1965 (Mehr 13, 1344 AHS), Imam, accompanied by his son Hajj Aqa Mustafa, left Turkey for his second place of exile: Iraq. There, he took up residence in the city of Najaf. In addition to his engagement in the teaching of courses in advanced studies of Islamic Jurisprudence (feqh) and presenting the theoretical bases of Islamic rule, which were later published in a book entitled Velayat-e Faqih orthe Government of the Islamic Jurisprudent, and despite the existing difficulties, Imam Khomeini assiduously monitored the political affairs of Iran and the world of Islam whilst in Najaf and maintained contact in various ways with the Iranian revolutionaries, the families of those martyred in uprising of June 5 (Khordad 15 AHS) and political prisoners. Imam's presence in Iraq presented the opportunity for the establishment of a more direct and improved connection with the believers and the Muslim students abroad than had existed in the past; and this very factor played a significant role in propagating Imam's ideas and the objectives of the struggle throughout the world.

With regard to the Arab-Israeli wars and the act of aggression perpetrated by the Zionist regime, Imam Khomeini put a great deal of effort into supporting the Palestinian Muslims' uprising and backing other front line countries.

Numerous meetings were held with the heads of militant Palestinian organizations; envoys were sent to Lebanon; and an important and historic religious decree (fatwa) was issued in which he declared it a religious duty to give military and economic support to the Palestinian uprising and those countries subject to invasion. These were just some of the actions that, for the first time, were taken by one of the world's prominent Shii maraje.

Imam's informative speeches and inspiring messages concerning the problems with Iran at a time when the Shah was at the peak of his par and was busy setting celebrations for 2,500 years of monarchical rule in motion and establishing a one-party system through the formation of the Rastakhiz Party, kept the flames of struggle burning. Imam's words of encouragement at this time were like balm to the wounds and iron to the resolve of the combatants who were undergoing barabaric forms of the torture in SAVAK's dark, dank dungeons and were condemned to long periods of imprisonment.

e) Culmination and Victory of the Islamic Revolution

The martyrdom of Imam's son, Ayatullah Hajj Aqa Mustafa Khomeini, on October 23, 1977 (Aban 1, 1956 AHS) was a watershed in the movement, and the huge ceremonies which took place in his memory throughout Iran marked the renewal of the uprising of the theological centers and the religious community in Iran. Imam Khomeini dealt with his son's death in a surprising manner, accepting it as one of God's blessings in disguise.

In revenge for the holding of these large memorial ceremonies, and the attacks which were made on the Shah in them, the regime published a scurrilous article against Imam in one of the country's state-run newspapers. Opposition to this article culminated in the uprising by the people of Qom on January 9, 1978 (Dey 19, 1356 AHS) during which a number of revolutionary religious students were killed. Once again the uprising had begun in the city of Qom and within a short space of time had spread to the rest of the country. Funeral ceremonies which, according to custom, took place on the third, seventh and fortieth day in commemoration of the death of the martyrs of this recent uprising, occured one after the other in Tabriz, Yazd, Jahrom, Shiraz, Isfahan and Tehran, spawning numerous revolts.

Throughout the whole of this period, Imam Khomeini's messages came thick and fast, and these along with the tape recordings of his speeches in which he called on the people to be steadfast and continue with their uprising until the foundations of the monarchical regime had been destroyed and an Islamic government established, were reproduced by his friends and followers and distributed on a wide scale throughout Iran. Despite resorting to the murder of crowds of people, the Shah could not quench the fire that had been kindled, and such tactics as announcing martial law in eleven cities, replacing the prime minister and changing officials in high positions also proved ineffective in stopping the spread of the revolution. All of the Shah's political and military manoeuvres were negated by the publication of Imam Khomeini's revelatory statements and militant directives.

A Summary of the Life and Struggles of Imam Khomeini

In a meeting between the Iranian and Iraqi foreign ministers in New York, the decision was made to expel Imam from Iraq. On September 24, 1978 (Mehr 2, 1357 AHS), Imam's home in Najaf was surrounded by Bathist forces. It was announced that his remaining in Iraq now depended on him stopping his political activities and relinquishing his struggle. Consequently, Imam's decision to continue with the fight led to his leaving Najaf, after thirteen years in exile there, on October 4, 1978 (Mehr 12, 1357 AHS), and heading for Kuwait. On arriving at the border, however, the Kuwaiti authorities, having been influenced by the Shah's regime, refused him entry. Thus, the Leader of the Revolution, after studying the situation in other Muslim countries and counsulting with his son, Hojjatol-Islam wal Muslemin Hajj Seyyed Ahmad Khomeini, decided to go to Paris.

Subsequently, on October 6 (Mehr 14) Imam entered Paris and two days later took up residence in the home of an Iranian in Neauphle-le-ChaÖteau on the outskirts of Paris. Representatives from the ElysÅes Palace communicated to him the French President's wish that he refrain from any kind of political activity while in France. Imam reacted sharply, making it clear that such restrictions were contrary to democratic principles and stating that even if he had to travel from airport to airport and country to country, he would not relinquish his aims.

Imam's four-month stay in France changed Neauphle-le-ChaÖteau into the most important news center in the world. His numerous interviews and meetings of different kinds with the many visitors who poured into the hamlet from all parts of the world meant that his views concerning an Islamic government and the future aims of the movement were made clearer for the people of the world.

On receiving the guidelines of Imam, the Iranian nation intensified their demonstrations, and through widening their strikes, paralyzed governmental organs and organizations. The replacement of prime ministers one after the other; the Shah's repentance for past offences; the regime's arrest and trial of old, infamous pawns; the freeing of political prisoners, and so on, went nowhere towards stopping the spread and intensification of the revolution.

The Leader of the Islamic Revolution sets up a Council of Revolution and informs the nation of its members. The Shah, on the pretext of feeling ill and needing a rest, flees the country on January 16, 1979 (Dey 26, 1357 AHS).

The news of the Shah's departure filled the nation with joy and strenghthened their resolve to continue the fight until the regime was destroyed. Imam's decision to return to the country created a wave of happiness and optimism that swept through the nation forcing the enemies of the revolution to react precipitously. After consultation with the American government, and with their cooperation, the regime closed the airports in the country to all foreign flights. As news of the closures reached the people, huge crowds from all parts of the country converged on Tehran and took part in the million-strong demonstrations staged by the people of Tehran to demand their reopening.

The regime gives in to the demands of the nation and opens Mehrabad airport in Tehran. Consequently, on February 12, 1979 (Bahman 12, 1357 AHS), after fourteen years in exile, Imam returns to his homeland.

The unprecedented welcome given Imam by the people of Iran was so huge and unequivocal that Western news agencies had no alternative but to recognize it for what it was; they put the figure of those attending at four to six million.

Despite the fact that the Shah's government was still in place, the Leader of the Revolution announced the formation of a provisional government and on February 5, 1979 (Bahman 16, 1357 AHS) with the appointment of a prime minister, he enjoined it to prepare the preliminaries for a referendom and the holding of elections.

On February 8 (Bahman 19), air force personnel went to the alavi School in Tehran, where Imam was staying, to pledge their allegiance to him. The following day (February 9/Bahman 20), soldiers from the Imperial Guard were dispatched to one of the most important air force bases in Tehran to quash a revolt by air force technicians (homafars) there. The people entered the arena to support the revolutionary forces and on February 10 (Bahman 21) police stations and government centers fell into the hands of the people one after the other.

Tehran's Military Command issues a proclamation extending curfew hours from 4 o'clock in the aftenoon so that the Shah's government, with the help of the American military advisers stationed in Tehran, can implement the prearranged plan for a coup d'Åtat. In a message, Imam Khomeini calls on the people of Tehran to take to the streets to prevent the impending plot from being carried out and to nullify martial law.

As a consequence, children, men and women, young and old alike, flood into the streets and set to building barricades. As soon as the first tanks and armored personnel carriers of the coup d'Åtat group leave their bases, they are immobilized by the people and the coup d'Åtat is faced with defeat at its very inception. In this way, the final resistance of the Shah's regime is broken and the sun of victory shines on the Islamic Revolution with the dawn of February 11, 1979 (Bahman 22, 1357 AHS).

f) The Formation of the Islamic Government and Its Outcome

The victory of the Islamic Revolution in Iran, and the fulfilment of Imam Khomeini's promises, was not an event confined purely to the domestic realm for a change in the political regime. Rather, just as many of the American, Israeli and European government officials noted in their memories of that time, the Islamic Revolution was like a destructive earthquake for the Western world. So it was that from the dawn of the morning of February 11, 1979 (Bahman 22, 1357 AHS), animosity towards the newly-established Islamic system began on a large scale from all directions.

The enemy front was led by America, while the British government and some of the other European governments, along with all the Western-dependent regimes, were active partners. The former Soviet Union and its satellites were also dissatisfied with the establishment of a religious government in Iran, and in many of the hostilities it sided with the Americans and helped them.

With the mobilization of the Iranian people for the reconstruction of the country, Imam Khomeini sought to present a model of a sound, advanced religious society to the rest of the world. For this reason, with the formation of an organization named the "Reconstruction Crusade" (jihad-e Sazandegi), he paved the way for the presence of thousands of experts and revolutionary forces in the villages and other deprived areas of the country, and in a short period of time, work began on the construction of roads, health centers and clinics and the supply of water and electricity on a wide scale.

Less than two months after the victory of the revolution, the Iranian people, in one of the freest elections ever held in the history of Iran, approved the establishment of an Islamic republic system by an overwhelming 98.2% of the votes. Following this, elections were held for the codification and approval of constitutional laws and the election of representatives for the Islamic Counsultative Assembly.

It was under these circumstances that the waves of sedition and foreign pressures swelled. By using fifth columnists, America sought to embroil The Islamic system in domestic problems and, by fanning the flames of dissent, pave the way for its demise. Amongst the first weapons used by the enemies of the revolution in their attempts to weaken the Islamic republic system was the assassination of prominent revolutionary figures. In a short period of time, such well-known personalities as the scholar Mortaza Motahari (a member of the Council of Revolution), Dr. Muhammad Mofateh, General Qarani (the Army Chief of Staff), Hajj Mahdi Araqi and Ayatullah Tabatabai were assassinated.

America not only gave a negative reply to the legitimate request of the Iranian for the Shah's return to Iran and the restitution of Iranian monies and assets in that country--which amounted to twenty-two billion dollars--but they also placed extensive facilities at the disposal of the supporters of the former Shah's regime who had fled the country so that they could organize themselves into opposition groups abroad. The anger of the Iranian nation at the open hostilities of America led to the occupation of the American Embassy in Tehran by a number of Iranian Muslim students. After defeating the resistance put up by the armed American guards there, the students arrested the American spies.

Imam Khomeini expressed his support for the students' revolutionary move, and described the take-over as a greater revolution than the first. The documents obtained from the embassy were gradually published in a series of more than seventy volumes entitled Documents from the American Espionage Den in Iran. These unassailable documents drew back the curtain on the secrets of American espionage activities in Iran and the numerous instances of American interference in the internal affairs of Iran and other countries of the world. They also revealed the names of many of the American agents, middlemen and spies, as well as the kinds of spying techniques employed and political incitements offered by this country in various regions of the world.

The occupation of the American Embassy, which in the lexicon of the Islamic Revolution has become known as the "espionage den", was a great humiliation for the governing body of that country. The most important achievements derived from this act in addition to guaranteeing the contiuation of the Islamic Revolution, were that it shattered the Pharaonic awesomeness which surrounded America and it gave hope to the nations of the third world as to the possibility of standing up to the big powers.

The defeat of the plans for the subversion of the Islamic Republic system, through the use of an economic and political blockade which was pursued by America, and this country's defeat in the Tabas desert operations which followed the occupation of the American espionage den, along with its failure to divide the country using the anti-revolutionary groups, set the American government thinking of a military solution. Consequently, on September 22, 1980 (Shahrivar 31, 1359 AHS), with American planning and the support of powerful countries, the Iraqi army began an extensive military assault along the 1,280 km common border with Iran, and at 2 o'clock in the afternoon of the same day, Iraqi fighter planes bombed Tehran airport and other areas.

Broadcast of the news of the start of Iraq's war against Iran, for all its importance, was accompanied by the deathly silence of all the international associations and all the powers worthy of mention in the world. Imam Khomeini's initial reactions and his first messages and speeches on the aggression of the Iraqi army, as regards his understanding and the kind of command he offered, are very interesting. However, their subtleties and special qualities are beyond the scope of this work. Be that as it may, his first reaction was to issue the command to resist, and in his first analysis given in a speech, he described America as the main agent behind the war as well as being Saddam's (the Iraqi president's) supporter and an instigator of the attack on Iran. He assured the people in no uncertain terms that if they rose up for God in defense of their land against the enemy's aggression and to carry out their religious duty, the enemy would most definitely be defeated, even though at that time everything seemed to point to the opposite.

The day after the Iraqi's first assault, Imam Khomeini, in a message to the Iranian nation, delineated the main lines to be adopted in administering war affairs and those of the country during wartime in seven short but very precise and comprehensive sections. Following this, in a number of messages to the Iraqi people and army, he issued an ultimatum, and from then on, the supervision and guidance of the difficult issue of the nation's eight-year-long defense of its lands began under unparalleled management. Imam's command for the mobilization of the people and the formation of a 20-million-strong army was welcomed by the revolutionary youth of Iran. Training began, volunteer forces were sent to the war fronts, and an air of spirituality suffused Iran. The successes of the soldiers of Iran's army came one after the other, and the signs of defeat became apparent on the enemy's front.

Eventually, the faces of America and her European allies began to appear from behind the war curtain. Different kinds of advanced weapons, the procurement of which, even in peacetime, was difficult and required years of constant effort, negotiations and concession giving, were placed at Saddam's disposal in no time at all. The extensive bombing of towns, cities, villages and economic centers, and the firing of destructive long-range missiles on residential areas resulting in the death of hundreds of women and children, were crimes which took place before the very eyes of the organizations claiming to defend human rights.

The multifarious help given Saddam in determining conditions on the war fronts, which were quickly turning in favor of the army of Islam, did not alter anything. As the bombing of residential areas and the missile attacks were intensified, America had no choice but to interfere directly. Battleships from France, Britain, America and the former Soviet Union entered the waters of the Persian Gulf. America saw the only remaining solution to lie in the internationalization of the war crisis and the direct involvement of other countries. Thus, the war known as the tanker war began.

The mission of the forces deployed in this war was to prevent the export of Iranian oil, to stop and inspect merchant ships, and to hinder the entry of basic goods into the Islamic Republic. In the course of this action, many Iranian merchant ships and oil tankers were subjected to missile and bomb attacks by American planes, and the oil wells belonging to Iran in the coastal waters of the Persian Gulf were set alight by American forces. In its final aggressive act against Iran, in July 1988 (Tir 1367 AHS), America perpetrated a shocking crime when one of its aircraft carriers shot down an Iranian passenger plane flying over the Persian Gulf killing all the 290 men, women and children on board. Another bitter event of this period was the massacre of Iranian pilgrims of the sacred House of God in Mecca by agents of the Saudi regime. On Friday, August 2, 1987 (Zol-Hajjah 6, 1407 AS/Mordad 11, 1366 AHS), when 150,000 pilgrims had taken to the streets of Mecca to participate in the Deliverance from Pagans ceremonies, street agents of the Saudi government along with the Saudi police placed obstacles across the main route of the demonstrators, and with prior readiness, they suddenly attacked them using different kinds of weapons. In this tragic event, approximately 400 pilgrims from Iran Lebanon, Palestine, Iraq and other countries were martyred, and around 5,000 people were injured, while a number of other innocent people were arrested. The majority of those martyred and injured were women and old people who could not escape the danger quickly enough.

The deployment of Western troops to the Persian Gulf, along with events which took place in the final months of the eight-year war, occured because the army of Islam was in a much better position, had pushed the enemy back across the border in most of the occupied territories and was continuing its advance to uproot the fundamental cause of calamity in the region. Saddam's downfall at the hands of the army of Islam would sound the drum of defeat for the world powers in their confrontation with the Islamic Republic, for contrary to the situation in the past, all the efforts of America and the Security Council were now turned to stopping the advance of the Iranian combatants and preventing Saddam's downfall.

The Iranian Government accepted Security Council resolution 598 containing most of Iran's conditions for an end to the hostilities. Imam Khomeini's message, which became famous as the message announcing acceptance of the resolution (July 20, 1988/Tir 29, 1367 AHS), is one of the masterpieces of his leadership in which a report of the imposed war and its dimensions was once again presented in clear terms. The future policies of the Islamic system and revolution in all areas including confirmation with the superpowers and remaining steadfast in the aims and aspirations of the revolution were also described therein.

In this way, the eight-year war came to an end. None of the aims behind its imposition had been achieved, and the honorable nation of Iran, under the prudent guidance of Imam, once again proved their rightfulness and deprived the enemy of their wish to divide and conquer Islamic Iran. In addition to the loss of vast human and economic resources which the two countries sustained in the war, the greatest crime and act of treachery which Saddam was responsible for, indeed one for which all the Arab, so-called "Islamic" governments who encouraged and helped him in his attack must also bear responsibility, is that with the imposition of this unwanted war, they delayed the uniting of the Islamic umma and the global Islamic Revolution--conditions for which were ripe from every aspect after the fall of the Shah--for many long years.

After the implementation of a partial peace, Imam Khomeini, in a speech delivered on October 3, 1988 (Mehr 11, 1367 AHS), addressed the officials of the Islamic Republic and delineated the policies for the reconstruction of the country in nine sections. A careful study of these instructions is sufficient to obtain a deep understanding of Imam's foresight while at the same time they show that Islamic values were his top priority.

Among the important acts of Imam Khomeini carried out in the last months of his life, and one worthy of reflection, is the dispatch of a letter to Mr. Gorbachev, the last head of the Union of Soviet Socialist Republics. In this letter, sent on January 1, 1989 (Dey 11, 1367 AHS), while analyzing the communism to manage the affairs of society and declared Russia's main problem to lie in its leader's lack of belief in God. In so doing, he also warned the Russian leadership against turning to the Western capitalist system and of being deceived by America. By propounding deep philosophical and gnostic matters and pointing out the failure of the communists in their anti-religion policies, Imam Khomeini in his letter asked

Mr. Gorbachev to turn to God and religion instead of pinning hopes on the materialism of the West.

One of the important and at the same time most odious of actions taken in these months was the publication and distribution of the book "The Satanic Verses" by publishers in Western countries. The support officially given the writer of this book, Salman Rushdie, by the Western governments can be taken as marking the start of the West's cultural assault on Islamic beliefs and values. The book questioned and attacked the fundaments of the Islamic faith and all that the Muslims hold sacred, their love for which has caused them to unite in their goals and has led to the recent Islamic movements. On February 14, 1989 (Bahman 25, 1367 AHS), Imam Khomeini, taking into account the existing realities and based on the Islamic doctrines which are accepted by all Muslim denominations and the formal legal opinions which are to be found in the juristical books of all the Islamic sects, issued a decree declaring Salman Rushdie an apostate and calling for his execution and that of the book's publishers who were aware of its blasphemous contents. With the issuance of such a decree, the Muslims, regardless of denomination, language and race, stood in serried ranks against this predetermined assault. The outcomes of this incident were to make manifest the existence of the Islamic community in the shape of a single nation (umma) and to show that whenever the Muslims are guided correctly, they can, despite their internal differences, play a determining role in the world's future as the forerunners of the movement for the revival of religious values.

In the years following the victory of the revolution, in the face of the movement plots hatched by the enemies of Islam--led by America--aimed at putting an end to the Islamic government in Iran, and despite the imposition of an eight-year war on the Muslim nation of Iran, Imam Khomeini, through his decrees and by presenting guidelines for the formation of new institutions and organizations as well as the restructuring the existing establishments--the remnants of the former regime--was able to pave the way for wide reaching and valuable services for the Iranian nation. The formation of institutions such as the Reconstruction Crusade, the Relief Committee, the Khordad 15 Foundation, the Housing Foundation, the Martyrs' Foundation, the Foundation for the Deprived and the Literacy Movement, to name but a few, which rendered services to the most remote areas of Iran and to the most deprived villages, is just one of the measures taken during the lifetime of His Holiness Imam Khomeini. The formation of the Islamic Revolution Committees, the Islamic Revolution Guard Corps, and the reorganization of the army, and the role these organizations played in establishing security, defending the country against the aggression of the Bathist regime and neutralizing the plots of the enemies, are amongst some of the most interesting and noteworthy developments of the Islamic Revolution.

Transforming the theological schools; changing and re-evaluating parts of the school and univeristy curricula; creating new university courses at different levels; establishing universities and centers of higher education in deprived cities; broadening the reception area of Iranian TV and radio broadcasts to include remote parts of the country, and providing said areas with communication services, are just some of the projects carried out at Imam's insistence and which he oversaw. The formation of a "Cultural Revolution Council" to supervise the planning of university courses, to compile textbooks for students and to train university lecturers, was a task undertaken in the early days after the victory of the Islamic Revolution.

After ten years of experience with the Islamic Republic system in Iran, and in order to reform and complete the pillars of the Islamic system, on April 24, 1989 (Ordibehesht 4, 1368 AHS), Imam Khomeini, in a letter to the president of the time (His Eminence Ayatullah Khamenei) called for a Council of Experts to be formed charged with the responsibility of looking into the reforms needed to the constititutional law and codifying them while bearing in mind the guidelines given in the letter. This decision and others like it show how important he considered strengthening the basis of the Islamic government to be, and how he used every available opportunity to prepare the grounds and pave the way for a better implementation of Islamic laws.

g) The Demise of the Supreme Leader of the Islamic Revolution

Although he was nearing ninety years of age, Imam Khomeini did not falter a moment in his efforts to elevate the Islamic community, and even at that age was still one of the most active political leaders in the world. Every day he not only studied the important news items and reports in the country's official newspapers, read dozens of news bulletins and listened to the news reports on domestic radio and television, but in addition he also turned in to the news reports and analyses of the foreign radio stations.

Imam firmly believed in the need for planning and having order and discipline in one's life. Certain hours of the night and day he spent in worship, prayer and reading the Quran. Taking walks while at the same time repeating words in praise of God and pondering matters formed a part of his daily routine. His cumulative, daily activities, along with his meetings with officials of the Islamic system, did not mean that his contacts with the ordinary people from all segments of the population were ignored, and up until the last week of his blessed life, he met with the families of the martyrs every week.

Even though he suffered from a heart disease, and in 1979 (1358 AHS) spent some time in the heart hospital in Tehran, what caused Imam Khomeini's departure from his ephemeral world was a disease of the digestive system. On the recommendations of the doctors treating him, he was operated on and after ten days in hospital, at 10.20 pm on Wednesday June 3, 1989 (Khordad 13, 1368 AHS) he bid farewell to this transitory world. The body of that great man was taken to the large prayer grounds in Tehran where it lay in state on the day and during the night of June 5 so that the martyr-nurturing nation of Iran could see their spiritual leader for the last time and say their farewells.

In an atmosphere of indescribable grief, millions of men and women clad in black, young and old alike from all over the country took part in the funeral ceremonies for that great man. The numbers participating were so great that even the Western news agencies had to acknowledge the magnificence of the affairs, and some of them even put the figure of mourners at more than 17 million. Imam's body was buried in an area close to Tehran's main cemetery, Behesht-e Zahra, where the martyrs of the revolution are buried. Following this, Islamic Iran spent a 40-day period lamenting the death of its father, and wherever you looked throughout the land, the black flags of mourning flew and groups of mourners beat their chests at the loss of the defender of Islamic values. The holy burial place of that dear person is now a site of pilgrimage for Muslims, freedom-seekers and independence-seekers from all over the world.

h) Children and Family

In 1929 (1308 AHS), His Holiness Imam married the daughter of the late Ayatullah Hajj Mirza Muhammad Thaqafi Tehrani. The fruits of this union were eight children: Mustafa (who later became the martyr Ayatullah Hajj Aqa Mustafa Khomeini); ali, who died at age four; Seddiqeh Mustafavi (who later became the wife of the now deceased Ayatullah Ishraqi); Farideh Mosfatavi (now the wife of Mr. Arabi); Fahimeh Mustafavi (also known as Zahra and married to Dr. Borujerdi); another daughter, Saedeh, who died when she was only eight months old; Ahmad (who became known as Hojjatol-Islam Hajj Ahmad Aqa Khomeini and who is now deceased); and finally, a daughter, Latifeh, who died in childhood.

A Summary of the Life and Struggles of Imam Khomeini

Even though throughout his struggle and political life, Imam relied only on God, sought help only from Him, and lent only on his faith in the steps he took, the active and effective role his son Hajj Aqa Mustafa played at his father's side throughout the Islamic movement did not go unnoticed by both the friends and foes of the revolution.

The organization of the revolutionary forces, gathering news and pertinent information, dispatching the secret messages of the Leader of the Revolution to the Grand Ayatullahs, the ulama and the leaders of the political groups, establishing contacts with revolutionary elements, etc. were just some of the activities that eventually led to his arrest by agents of the Shah's regime. His very existence was viewed by the Pahlavi regime's security organization as a danger, and as a result, upon his release from prison, he, like his great father before him, was sent into exile first in Turkey then Iraq. For sure, the reason behind his martyrdom in 1977 (1356 AHS) was nothing other than the influential role he played in shaping and perpetuating the Islamic movement.

The responsibility which, until that date, Hajj Aqa Mustafa had been predestined to shoulder, now passed into the hands of his young but capable brother Hajj Ahmad Aqa. Prior to this unpleasant incident, Hajj Ahmad Aqa had been busy studying at the theological schools, and this was, on the face of it, all he did. However, secretly he bore the same responsibilities as his brother discharging them in the theological schools in Qom and other areas of Iran. When Imam's house in Najaf was transformed into the revolution's control center and the base from which it was exported, it was he who was charged with the duty of running the affairs of the house; planning the meetings of the Leader of the Revolution; establishing necessary contacts with Najaf for the combatants; preparing reports on the broadening of the revolutionary activities in Iran and presenting them to Imam; communicating Imam's directives to the combatants and also establishing broad contacts with the militant groups in the country.

Throughout those sensitive days when the struggle of the Muslim people was gaining momentum, during the period following the migration of the Leader of the Revolution to France, on the return of that great man to his Islamic homeland and following the victory of the revolution, Hajj Ahmad Aqa was a skillful adviser, a prudent politician, an untiring fighter, an intelligent custodian, a confidant, and a devoted disciple in the service of his father. He concentrated all his efforts on attaining his father's satisfcaction in order to obtain God's satisfaction. Hajj Ahmad Aqa's unequalled role at the side of the effulgent flame of the beloved Imam's existence was a wellspring of blessings the effects of which can be seen in all areas of the history of the Islamic Revolution.

After the death of His Holiness Imam, Hojjatol-Islam wal-Muslemin Hajj Ahmad Aqa, in order to serve the Islamic republic system and the revolution, spent part of his time assisting a number of political and cultural organs where he was engaged in presenting guidelines and discharging his responsibilities. As one of the salient personalities of the revolution, he became adviser to the leadership and the officials of the system.

In order to protect the written works and speeches of the Supreme Leader of the Islamic Revolution and to publish the thoughts and ideas of that great man, Hajj Ahmad Aqa took upon himself the responsibility of setting up the Institute for Compilation and Publication of the Works of Imam Khomeini. In addition, he devoted a great deal of unceasing effort to transforming the holy shrine of Imam into a source of inspiration for the Islamic Revolution. At the time of Hajj Ahmad Aqa's demise, brought on by a heart complaint (March 17, 1995/Isfand 26, 1373 AHS), the Institute for Compilation and Publication of the Works of Imam Khomeini had obtained the importance it deserved and the holy shrine complex was accorded the esteem and value befitting such a holy place. According to the wishes of Hajj Ahmad Aqa, as laid down in his will, trusteeship of the shrine and the institute was passed onto his eldest son Hojjatol-Islam wal-Muslemin Hajj Seyyed Hassan Khomeini so that Imam's path would always be lucid and the memory of that dear man would remain eternal.

Imam's way of life, its simplicity and lack of extravagance, had its roots in his religious beliefs, and throughout the different periods in his life, during the highs and lows of the political struggle and under the various circumstances: the years in prison, in exile, of migration and victory, it remained unchanged. Correspondents from the famous foreign newspapers and news agencies of the world, who, after the death of Imam, were given permission to enter the place he had called home for the last years of his life to gather information for their reports, were surprised at how modest it was and how simple the life of the Supreme Leader of the Islamic Revolution had been, noting that it was in no way comparable to the current lifestyles of the heads of state and political and religious leaders of other countries. His lifestyle was reminiscent of that of the messengers of God and of other holy people.

i) The Literary Works and Compilations of Imam Khomeini (pbuh)

Dozens of valuable books and literary works by Imam Khomeini on such subjects as ethics, gnosticism, jurisprudence, principles of religion, philosophy, as well as political and social matters remain, a number of which have not yet been published. Unfortunately, some of his valuable treatises and compilations were lost during removal from one rented accommodation to another and as a result of the attack of the Shah's SAVAK agents on his house and library. Following is a list of his works and compilations in the order in which they were written. Each one of them really requires a detailed explanation, however, this is beyond the scope of this biography:

1. Sharh-e Doa-ye Sahar
2. Sharh-e Hadith-e Rasol-Jalut
3. Hashiyeh-ye Imam bar Sharh-e Hadith-e Rasol-Jalut
4. Hashiyeh bar Sharh-e Fawaedol Rezwayah
5. Sharh-e Hadith-e Jonud-e aql wa Jahl
6. Mesbahol Hedaya ela Khalafa wal Welayat
7. Hashiyeh bar Sharh-e Fosusol Hokm
8. Hashiyeh bar Mesbahol-Ens
9. Sharh-e Chehel Hadith
10. Serrol-Salah (Salahol-Arefin wal Mirajol-Salekin)
11. Adabol-Salah
12. Resalah-ye Laqaollah
13. Hashiyeh bar Asfar
14. Kashfol-Asrar
15. Anwarol-Hedaya fel-Taliqat alol-Kafiyah (two volumes)
16. Badaiyol-Durar fi Qaeda nafi-ol-Zarar
17. Resalatol-Istes-hab
18. Resalah fel-Taadol wal Tarajih
19. Resalatol-Ijtihad wal Taqlid
20. Manahejol-Wosul ela Elmol-Osul (two volumes)
21. Resalah fel-Talab wal Eradah
22. Resalah fel-Taqiyah
23. Resalah fi Qaedah men Moluk
24. Resalah fi Tayeenol-Fajr fel-Leyali-ol Moqamerah
25. Ketabol-Taharah (four volumes)
26. Taliqah ala-ol-Urwatol-Wotqa
27. Makasib-e Mohremah (two volumes)
28. Taliqatol-Wasilatol-Najdah

29. Resalah Najahollbad
30. Hashiyeh bar Resala-ye Erth
31. Taqrirat-e Dars-e Osul-e Ayatullahol-Ozma Borujerdi
32. Tahrirol-Wasilah (two volumes)
33. Ketabol-Bey (five volumes)
34. Hokumat-e Islami (Velayat-e Faqih)
35. Ketabol-Khelal fi al-Salha
36. Jihad-e Akbar ya Mobarezeh ba Nafs
37. Taqrirat-e Dorus-e Imam Khomeini
38. Towzihol Masa-el (Practical Treatise)
39. Tafsir-e Sura-ye Hamd
40. Isteftayat
41. Divan-e Sher
42. Name-ha-ye Irfani
43. Last Will and Testament

The 22 volumes of the *Sahifeh-ye Imam* series, constitute the most comprehensive collection of Imam's speeches, messages, interviews, decrees, religious permissions, and letters.

That which is presented after this introduction is Imam Khomeini's last will and testament which is of a religio-political nature and which, according to the Islamic tradition and in keeping with the ways of the prophets and pious people, he wrote a few years before his demise, so that his passing, like his life, may inspire awakening, awareness and movement.

May peace be upon you and the mercy and blessings of God.

Last Message

Explanation on the manner of writing the Last Testament of Imam Khomeini:

Imam Khomeini finished writing his politico-religious testament, which is indeed his everlasting message and summary of all testaments and messages of his blessed life on Bahman 26, 1361 AHS [February 15, 1983]. In the course of a message dated Tir 22, 1362 AHS [July 13, 1983], he entrusted a sealed copy of it to the first Assembly of Experts. Several years later, Imam Khomeini reviewed his last testament. By making changes in it, he entrusted two copies of the edited text to his representatives. On the envelopes the Imam's hand writing read: "The text of my politio-religious testament for safekeeping with the Assembly of Experts and Imam Rida's Holy Shrine" to be handed over to the mentioned centers. To submit the copies of the testament, ceremonies were held by a group of officials of the Islamic Republic of Iran on Azar 19, 1366 AHS [December 10, 1987]. The Islamic Republic of Iran Broadcasting (IRIB) covered the ceremony. Present at the ceremony were Messrs. Muntaziri (the then Deputy Supreme Leader), Khamenei (President), Hashimi Rafsanjani (Speaker of the Islamic Consultative Assemlby), Mir Husayn Musawi (Prime Minister), Mishkini (Chairman of the Assembly of Experts), Safi (Secretary of the Guardian Council), Musawi Ardebili (Chief Justice), Musawi Khuiniha (General Public Prosecutor), Mahdawi-Kani (Secretary of the Society of Combatant Clergy), Karrubi (Secretary of the Assembly of Combatant Clerics), Sayyid Ahmad Khomeini and members of in Imam Khomeini's Office. After the meeting, those present went to the Islamic Consultative Assembly for sealing the testament. At the presidential room, Mr. Mishkini first delivered a speech and then Sayyid Ahmad Khomeini submitted the testament to him. The sealing ceremony took place in the presence of the group. Messrs. Mahdawi-Kani, Karrubi, Tawassuli, and Sanai carried the copy to Imam Rida's Holy Shrine in the Holy city of Mashhad. The previous copy kept with the Assembly of Experts was sent to the Imam by Sayyid Ahmad Khomeini.

Politico-Divine Will

In the Name of God, the Compassionate, the Merciful

His Holiness Muhammad, the Prophet of Allah (*s*) has said: "*I leave among you the Thaqalayn:*[1] *the Book of Allah and my Itrah.*[2] *Verily, they will be inseparable from each other until they join up with me at the Howd.*[3]"
To Allah belongs all praises and thanks and hallowed be Thou. *O' Allah, bless Muhammad (s) and his household who are manifestations of Thy Beauty and Magnanimity and the treasures of secrets of Thy Book, which crystallizes Thy Oneness through all Thy Glorious Names even the Supreme One that no one knows other than Thee. Curse be upon those belonging to the root of evil tree that transgressed upon them (the Prophet and his progeny).*

To being this prologue, it is apropos to touch on the two most exalted and precious things (the *Thaqalayn*). My explanation does not dwell on the transcendental, spiritual or mystical aspects of the *Thaqalayn*. It is a domain, the cognition of which covers all circles of beings, from earth to heaven and beyond to His Divine Presence including circles that lie beyond our comprehension. Nor do I mean to comment on that which has befallen humanity by his negligence of the true nature and status of the greater trust or precious thing, i.e. *Thiql-e Akbar* (the Holy Quran) and that of the great trust, i.e. *Thiql-e Kabir* (the progeny of the Prophet—*s*) which is greater than anything except *Thiql-e Akbar* which is absolutely great. Nor will this explanation speak of the harm that enemies of Allah and the *Taghuti*s[4] have done to these two *theqls*, for it is impossible for someone like me, with

---

[1] The term '*Thaqalayn*' means 'two *thiql*s'. The term '*thiql*' is used in explanatory accounts of traditions and narratives as well as in interpretations of the Holy Quran in various senses and concepts such as 'weighty heritage', 'great thing', 'a precious thing', 'an invaluable trust', etc. However, in the *Thaqalayn* narration, by the two precious things it is meant the Holy Quran and the Holy Prophet's household.
[2] Members of the Prophet's family.
[3] '*Hawd*' means a pool, pond or ditch dug in the ground to store water. In Islamic literature, the term '*Hawd*' usually precedes the word '*kawthar*'. According to narratives, it means the *Kawthar* Pond, a stream located in Paradise.
[4] The term '*Taghutis*' means followers of *Taghut*, a term used in the Quran on various occasions. *Taghut* was also the name of an idol of the Qoraysh tribe in pre-Islamic days. This name has also been used to mean Satan, oppressor, tyrant and dictatorial governments.

limited knowledge and time to give an account of all the wrongs done to the *Thaqalayn* by the *Taghuti*s and the enemies of Allah. I only considered it appropriate to summarize the sufferings which the two *theql*s have endured.

Perhaps the phrase *"they will be inseparable"* is an indication that, after the passing away of the Holy Prophet (*s*), whatever has happened to one of these two *thiql*s has also happened to the other. Once one is left abandoned, the other is left abandoned too. Until these two abandoned theqls join the Prophet of Allah (*s*) at the *Howd*. This *Howd*, however, may be the similitude of the station at which multiplicity connects to the unity. It may imply merging of droplets in an ocean or anything else, which is incomprehensible by the intellect and understanding of human beings. Moreover, the cruelty which these two Divine trusts have suffered, was also imposed on the Islamic nation and even the entire humanity. The transgression wrought by tyrants and their stooges defy description by pen.

The concatenate Hadith of Thaqalayn[1] has been quoted by both Shiite and Sunni schools as a positive proof for mankind, especially for Muslims. References to this noble had ith are frequently made in such reliable Sunni sources like the famous 'Six Correct Texts' [2] as well as in countless cogent Shiite texts. *Thaqalayn Hadith* has been narrated in several occasions by the Holy Prophet (*s*). This tradition has been accepted as an irrefutable proof for all Muslims regardless of their schools of thought. For the Muslims who are informed of this tradition, it is incumbent to act upon it. If there is an excuse for the uninformed, there is none for the scholars of the various schools of thought.

Now, let us see what has befallen to the Book of Allah, this Divine trust and legacy of the Prophet of Islam (*s*). The sad events, for which tears may well be shed, began to take place following the martyrdom of Imam Ali (*s*). [3]

---

[1] In Islamic teachings, it means words and sayings as definitely coming from the companions of the Prophet (*s*) or the Infallible Imams (*s*).
[2] These six correct volumes which the learned Sunni authorities and jurists selected from among the many volumes of traditions and designated them as the base and source from which to deduce religious laws, tenets, commands, interpretations and a part of the history of the early days of Islam.
[3] Ali (*s*), the first Infallible Imam of Shiite Muslims, was born 600 A.D. to Fatimeh daughter of Asad and Abutalib paternal uncle of the Prophet (*s*). Ali (*s*) grew up in the house of the Prophet (*s*) since the age of 6. He was the first male person who embraced Islam and pledged himself to assist the Prophet (*s*). When the Prophet (*s*) called his own kins to Islam early in his Prophetic mission, he announced at a gathering attended by his relatives: "The first among you to believe in and accept my faith shall succeed me." He repeated this sentence three times and each time Ali (*s*) was the only person who professed his faith. On the night of hejira

Selfish people and followers of *Taghut*s abused the Holy Quran as a means by which to establish anti-Quranic rules.

To achieve this mischievous target, they forced off the scenes the true interpreters of the Quran as well as those who had received all of the Holy Book directly from the Prophet (*s*) and their ears still echoed with the voice of His Holiness Muhammad (*s*) who declared: "... *I leave among you the Thaqalayn* ..." Thus, by abusing the Holy Quran, which was to be man's guide to moral and material life to the Last Day, was shelved and the rule of Divine justice that is one of the doctrines of the Holy Book was into oblivion. They laid the foundation for deviation from the religion of Allah, the Holy Book and the Tradition to the point that pen is ashamed to explain.

The more this deviated trend advanced, the more the Holy Quran, which has been sent down by the Almighty God for guidance of mankind, was forced out of the scene. The Holy Book, which was descended to guarantee the progress of mankind, to bring unity not only among Muslims but also among entire humankind, to deliver mankind to its final destination, to liberate the offsprings of Adam to whom Allah has taught the names of objects, to permit the entire existence to achieve justice and equity and to hand over the government to 'the Infallible Imams' in order that they, in turn, leave it to those who would rule for the good of the entire humanity, was so forced out of the scene that it appeared to have no role to play in guiding mankind. This deviation reached a point where the role of the Glorious Quran in the hands of the oppressive rulers and their wicked clerics who were more corrupt than the *Taghuti*s, was distorted and abused as an instrument to continue their oppression and corruption and to justify the

---

(migration of the Prophet—*s* from Mecca to Medina), Ali (*s*) lay down in the Prophet's bed to foil the plot woven by the enemy to kill the prophet in his bed.

The Quraysh had plotted to assassin the Prophet (*s*) that night and Ali (*s*) thus demonstrated his fidelity to the prophet (*s*), who adopted Ali (*s*) as his own brother; on return from his Last Hajj pilgrimage (at a place called *Ghadir*, where the Prophet) *s* (publicly declared Ali (*s*) as the guardian of the Muslims and administrator of their affairs. Ali (*s*) was a companion of the Prophet (*s*) in his lonely days and his assistant in hardships and dangers.

For a period of 25 years after the Prophet's demise, Ali (*s*) was deprived of government administration and leadership by his opponents. After the third Caliph was killed, the companions and a number of other people swore allegiance to Ali (*s*) and selected him as the fourth Caliph. Imam Ali (*s*) administered the affairs of the Islamic world for nearly four years and nine months. He restored the changes that had occurred after death of the Prophet (*s*). The dissidents whose interests were threatened, rose on every side and, pretending to avenge the blood of the 3rd Caliph, set off bloody internal wars that lasted during the entire period of Ali's (*s*) rule, until, finally, they martyred this unique man of history next to the Prophet (*s*) in the altar where he was performing prayers.

wrong doings of the enemies of Allah. Unfortunately, the Glorious Quran, which is capable of helping mankind to find his path in life, was not given a role other than to be recited in cemeteries because of plots of its mischievous enemies as well as ignorant friends. So, this Holy Book, which was to be the source of unity and guidance for man's life, was either used as a means to generate discord and conflict or totally driven out of the scene. We witnessed that if anyone spoke of an Islamic government or politics, which according to Quran and Tradition is the major role of Islam and the Prophet (s), one would be treated as if one had committed the greatest sin. The label 'politicized cleric' was made to parallel 'irreligious cleric'. This wrong concept still persists in certain groups and governments throughout the world.

Recently, satanic superpowers by employing anti-Islamic governments have deceptively attached themselves to Islam, have published that beautifully designed Qurans and dispatched volumes all over the world for the sole purpose of forcing out the Holy Quran from the scene and, thus attaining their satanic objectives. One of the examples that we all observed is the Quran published by Muhammad Reza Pahlavi [1] and, thereby succeeded in deceiving some people including a few Muslim clerics and preachers who, being unaware of the aims of Islam, praised him for it. Now, we witness Malik Fahad [2] spends regularly enormous sums of the people's wealth on publishing certain versions of the Holy Quran and supporting anti-Quranic ideas to propagate the baseless and superstitious dogmas of Wahhabism. [3] He abuses the Quran and urges negligent people and nations to side with the superpowers. Thus, he uses the noble Islam and the Holy Quran to destroy both.

---

[1] The king of Iran.
[2] King Fahad is the king of Saudi Arabia. The extent of Al-e Saud's dependence on major powers, especially on the world-mongering America, the role of this family in the spread of the false and pervert creed of Wahhabism, their ancient historic animosity towards the followers of Ali (s), their hypocritical approach towards the fighting people of Palestine, their massacre of the pilgrims of Iran and other countries in the House of God, their intrusion on the Divine sanctuaries, suppression of the Arab strugglers in and out of Saudi Arabian Peninsula, squandering the wealth of the Muslims ... and other atrocities of this family are all known to the whole world.
[3] Wahhabism was founded by Muhammad Bin Abdul-Wahhab Najdi toward the end of the 12th and the early 13th century A.H. and is ascribed to British colonialism. The adherents of Wahhabism are of the opinion that all Islamic sects, are idol worshippers. They regard respect and reverence toward the shrine of the Prophet (s) and the Infallible Imams (s) a kind of heresy and paganism. Supported by Muslim wealth, the Wahhabis are active in cultural propaganda; they are instruments for implementation of the destructive plans of the superpowers.

We and our dedicated nation are proud that we adhere to a religion, in which the Holy Quran speaks of unity of all Muslims and the oneness of mankind. We are proud that our faith has retrieved the Quran from the cemeteries and saved this Holy Book, which is the best prescription for liberating human beings from all physical, mental and intellectual chains shaking their hands, feet, hearts and minds and dragging them towards non-existence, destruction, slavery and subjugation under the *Taghuti*s.

We are honored that we follow the religion established by the Command of Allah through His Prophet (*s*). We are proud that we are the followers of Imam Ali (*s*) the embodiment of a man detached from all worldly chains, ones who was, in turn, appointed as the liberator of mankind from all chains of slavery.

We are honored that Nahjol Balagheh,[1] as a religious guiding book next the Glorious Quran and as the most elevated constitution for spiritual and material life and the greatest book for liberation of mankind together with its political guidelines, is authored by Ali (*s*), our Infallible Imam.

We are honored that the twelve Infallible Imams [2] from Ali Bin Abitalib (*s*) to Imam Mahdi [3] (May God hasten his glad advent) the Savior of mankind

---

[1] A religious guiding book by Imam Ali (*s*). The contents of this book revolve around the three essential subjects of God, the universe and man, comprising scientific, literary, religious, social, ethical and political topics. Next to the words of the Holy Quran and statements by the Prophet (*s*), no words regardless of the source and author, can equate those of the Nahjol-Balagheh in significance and eloquence. So far more than 101 exegeses and commentaries have been written about the Nahjol-Balagheh, indicating the importance of this book to the authorities in science, research and study.

[2] Explicit Islamic texts indicate that after the Prophet (*s*), the holy leaders and infallible caliphs of the Prophet known as Imams number 12. They are:
1. Ali ibn Abitalib - Imam Ali (*s*).
2. Hasan Bin Ali - Imam Hasan (*s*).
3. Husayn Bin Ali -Imam Hossein (*s*).
4. Ali Bin Hossein-Imam Sajjad (*s*).
5. Muhammad Bin Ali - Imam Muhammad Baqir (*s*).
6. Jafar Bin Muhammad - Imam Jafar Sadiq (*s*).
7. Musa Bin Jafar - Imam Musa Kazim (*s*).
8. Ali Bin Musa - Imam Rida (*s*).
9. Muhammad Bin Ali - Imam Muhammad Taqi (*s*).
10. Ali Bin Muhammad - Imam Ali Naqi (*s*).
11. Hasan Bin Ali - Imam Hasan Askari (*s*).
12. Hujjat Bin al-Hasan - Imam Mahdi (May God hasten his reappearance).

[3] The era of leadership of the 12th Shiite Imam, His Holiness Hujjat Bin al-Hasan Askari (May God hasten his reappearance) began when he was only 6 years old. Because of the conditions prevailing at the time and by Allah's will, His Holiness went into occultation. The period of occultation of Imam Mahdi (May God hasten his reappearance) is divided into two

who by the grace of Allah lives in occultation, and supervises and watches our doing, are all our leaders.

We feel honored by our Infallible Imams who have authored such exalted and life-giving supplications as the Shabaniyeh Orisons;[1] the Arafat Prayer of Imam Husayn (s);[2] the *Sahifeh-ye Sajjadiyeh*,[3] known as the Zabur [4] (psalms) of the Household of Muhammad (s) and the Sahifeh-ye Fatimiyeh, [5] revealed by Allah to Her Holiness Fatimeh Zahra (s).

---

parts: the lesser and the grand occultation. The lesser or minor occultation lasted 69 years. During this period, His Holiness was indirectly in communion with the people through the medium of four representatives. Then began the grand or major occultation which has continued to this date and will be effective until his reappearance and the triumph of Truth over falsehood. Islamic thought holds to the view that the extensive challenges of Imam Mahdi (*a*) and his impending reappearance would be the last link in the chain of the fights of supporters of Truth against adherents of falsehood. This means that the struggles of the followers of Truth will continue throughout history and that grounds for the victory of Truth become better prepared with each day passing and culminate in the reappearance and rise of the Promised Mahdi (*a*) with the eventual dawn of the light of Truth and justice in man's horizons, marking his intellectual, moral, and social maturity.

[1] Because of richness of contents and importance, this invocative litany has been frequently recited during the month of Shaban by Imam Ali (*s*) and other Infallible Imams. On the importance of this prayer as often emphasized by Imam Khomeini in the course of his blessed life, suffice it to say that no other invocation is said to have been recited by all the Infallible Imams (*s*)

[2] Arafat is a station for Hajj pilgrims in the vicinity of Mecca. The Prayer of Arafat is ascribed to Imam Husayn (*s*) and was often recited by him and Imam Sajjad (*s*) on the 19th of the month of Dhu'l-Hijjah in the desert of Arafat. This prayer is expressive of the lovely supplications made by the Master of Martyrs (Imam Husayn - *s*) invoking the mercy of his beloved God, the One and only Creator of universe. The Arafat Prayer, contains deep and lofty concepts as does other prayers of the Infallible Imams (*s*).

[3] In view of the dominance of tyranny in time of Imam Sajjad (*s*), the fourth leader of the Shiite Muslims of the world, a collection of his advices, exhortations and counsellings have been handed down to us in the form of prayers and supplications. This collection which contains 54 of such entries is known as the *Sahifeh-ye Sajjadiyeh*; it is a veritable encyclopedia that has been constantly referred to us a source of inspiration to Muslims and seekers of the Path of Allah in the course of history of Shi'ism. This book has a great impact on the readers through its educational influence.

[4] *Zabur* is the name of a Divine Book that was sent down to His Holiness Davud (David), a great Prophet of Allah. It contains plenty of phrases and sayings of knowledge and wisdom. The *Sahifeh-ye Sajjadiyeh* is also known as "the *Zab ur* of the family of Mohammad".

[5] The word '*Sahifeh*' means letter or book. The term '*Fatimiyeh*' implies the realities and topics ascribed to Her Holiness Fatimeh (*s*). Thus the *Sahifeh-ye Fatimiyeh* is a book attributed to Fatimeh Zahra, daughter of our noble Prophet (*s*) and consort to Ali (*s*), man of equity and virtue and the first Imam of Shiites. Fatimeh is the mother of Imams Hasan and Husayn (*s*), who are the 2nd and the 3rd Shia leaders. She was born in Mecca in the 2nd or the 5th year after divinely appointment of Mohammad (*s*) to Prophetic mission. Comment on the qualities and attributes of Fatimeh, this grand lady of Islam and symbol of Muslim woman, is

We are honored that Baqirul-Olum [1] the fifth Infallible Imam, who is the highest personality of history in the domain of Divine knowledge, belongs to us. His station is known only by Almighty God, the Holy Prophet (s) and the Infallible Imams.

We are honored that we follow the Jafari school of thought [2] and that our jurisprudence (*fiqh*), [3] which is the infinite ocean of knowledge, is from Imam Jafar Sadiq (s). We are proud of all our Infallible Imams (pbut) and devoted to following them.

We are honored that all of our Infallible Imams (pbut), who suffered in prisons and exiles, finally became martyrs as a result of attempting to eradicate oppressive governments and *Taghut*s of their own time in order to raise the status of Islam and to implement the teachings of the Holy Quran, one of whose aspects is to establish a just government. Today, we are honored that we are determined to implement the concepts of the Glorious Quran and those of the Traditions. Our people, with outpouring enthusiasm sacrificed their lives, properties and beloved ones in the way of Allah.

We are honored that our women, young and old, prominent or unknown, attend cultural, economic and military scenes side by side with men or sometimes more active than men in raising the status of Islam and achieving the goals of the Holy Quran. Those, who have the ability to fight, take courses in military training program, which is obligatory in defense of Islam and the Islamic nation. Our women have liberated themselves from the deprivations imposed on them, on Islam and Muslims by the enemies of

---

beyond the scope of this writing. Her love and attachment to her father was so intense that people called her 'Umma Abiha' (her father's mother). Fatimeh (s) was a helper of the Prophet (s) and Ali (s) during the most eventful terms of their Divine mission. She passed away young because of the great pain and hardship she went through following the death of her father, the Holy Prophet of Allah (s).

[1] The term 'baqir' means 'splitter' or 'dissector' and Baqirul-Olum or Dissector of Sciences and Knowledge was a title accorded to the 5th Imam or the leader of the Shiite Muslims of the world. This title which is a proved prophecy was given to him before his birth by the Prophet of Allah (s).

[2] The Jafari religion or Jafari Islamic School of Thought is attributed to Imam Jafar Sadiq (s), the sixth leader of the world of Shiism. He extended the means of teaching Islamic truths and arranged classes for lessons, discussions and debates and also succeeded in furthering the education of the faithful believers and the establishment of a great theological center.

[3] *Fiqh* is a science dealing with deduction of religious rules and the practical aspects of religion for every individual in his private and social life. The objective of this science is understanding the Divine commands and acting according to them. The sources from which *fiqh* deduces Allah's Commands include: Holy Quran, Tradition of the Prophet (s) and of that Infallible Imam (s); consensus among the Islamic learned men about issues the correctness of which cannot be doubted, and reason.

Islam and by inadequate knowledge of friends of Islamic tenets and the Holy Quran. They have bravely discarded the superstitions created by enemies through some ignorant clerics. Those women who are unable to fight have served behind the front lines with such distinction and valor that has thrilled the heart of the nation with joy and delight while making the hearts of the enemies and the ignorants, who are worse than the enemies, tremble with anger and frustration. We have repeatedly witnessed that our honorable women cry out, as did venerable Zeynab (s), [1] that they are proud of losing their sons in the way of Allah and the beloved Islam and that they are willing to sacrifice everything they have. They well know that what they have earned is higher than the blessed Paradise as a reward, not to mention the cheap worldly belongings.

Not only our nation but also the entire Muslim community as well as all of the oppressed people of the world are proud of the fact that their enemies, who are the enemies of Allah, the Holy Quran, and the beloved Islam are the ones who ferociously commit any crime or treason to achieve their gastly criminal purposes. The chief among these enemies, who does not distinguish friends from foes in obtaining power and satisfying greed, is America. This master of international terrorism by nature has set fire to everything and everywhere. The US close ally is the international Zionism that commits such crimes that are too shameful to be mentioned by tongues or written by pens in order to achieve its greedy ends. The Zionists idiotic fantasy of 'Greater Israel' [2] urges them to commit all types of crime. The Muslim

---

[1] Zeynab-e-Kubra (the Great Zeynab), the brave lady of Islam is the third child of Imam Ali (s) and Fatimeh Zahra (s) after Imam Hasan (s) and Imam Husayn (s). She was born in the 6th year A.H. and Fatimeh nurtured and raised under the care and education of the Prophet (s), Ali (s) and Fatimeh (s) like her two brothers. Zeynab's (s) traverse was an eye-witness to the long thorny passage up to the tragedy of Karbala. In that great tragedy, Zeynab (s) was an eye-witness to the martyrdom of her holy brother Imam Husayn (s) and other young men of her family. She traveled to Iraq in captivity and then to Sham (Syria) and supervised the remaining family members of Imam Husayn (s). During this tragic event, Zeynab did not, for a moment, lose her fortitude and patience. She managed to create a center to vent their anger and wrath against Yazid, the blood-thirsty Umayyeh Caliph. With unique courage, she hoisted the banner of challenge against the criminals. By performing an awe-inspiring role, she took the initial steps toward perpetuation of the epical deeds of Imam Hussein and his companions in Ashura and the struggle of truth against falsehood in all ages.

[2] The only ideal and objective in which the Zionists strongly believe is the formation of Jewish government to exercise sovereign rule over the entire world. According to them, such a government will rise from Palestine and would extend to the Egyptian territory between the Nile and the Red Sea Sina, Jordan, Syria, the greater part of Iraq with a window opening to the Persian Gulf and the western part of the Saudi domain. Because of the immeasurable natural

community and the oppressed people of the world are proud that their enemies are Husayn of Jordan, [1] this vulgar professional criminal, Hasan of Morocco [2] and Husni Mubarak of Egypt, [3] who are all allies of the criminal Israel and who commit any treason against their own people in order to serve America and Israel. We are proud that our enemy is Aflaqi Saddam, whose friends and enemies alike consider him a criminal and a violator of human rights. Everyone knows that his acts of treason against the oppressed people of Iraq and the Sheikhdoms of the Gulf are no less than what he has committed against the Iranian nation.

We and the oppressed people of the world are proud that the mass media and the world propaganda apparatus accuse us of any crime and treason that the criminal superpowers dictate to them to propagate. What can be a better source of pride than that the US government with all its war equipment and military might, boastfulness, claims, allies among puppet regimes, all the wealth it has stolen from the oppressed countries of the world and control over mass media has become so disgraced. It is helpless to face the brave nation of Iran, the hand of the Savior (May God hasten his glad advent). The US has become so desperate that it does not know to which way and to whom to turn. This is not but with assistance of Almighty God, Who has awakened all nations, particularly the Muslim Iranian nation and guided the nation from darkness into the light of Islam.

I now take this opportunity to advise oppressed and noble nations, including our people, to stay firmly on this Divine straight path that leads neither to the atheistic East nor to the oppressive West, but to the path that Almighty God has decreed for us. I further advise not to neglect in thanksgiving for this blessing even for a single moment. They should not let the polluted hands of superpowers and their agents, whether domestic or

---

resources which they shall thus acquire, they think and believe that sovereignty over this area is sovereignty over the entire world.

[1] The present king of Jordan, known as Malik Husayn has taken a stand beside the Saudi Arabian monarchy, the reactionary Arab rulers and Saddam as of the victory of Islamic Revolution, challenging the Islamic Revolution. Hussein's betrayal of the ideals of the people of Palestine, bloody massacre of Palestinians and his support of Israel have made him a hated figure among Muslims.

[2] Shah Sultan Hasan II, the monarch of Morocco is one of the despotic kings who, like the king of Jordan and Arabia considers the collapse of the previous regime of Iran and the formation of the Islamic government, a major threat to their thrones. He has not spared any mischievous action in opposition to the Islamic Revolution of Iran.

[3] Mubarak is the current president of Egypt who, after the terror of the treacherous Anwar Sadat, goes on with the shameful Camp David Treaty and the humiliating peace with Israel. He is a sworn servant of America.

foreign, affect your intentions and determination. They should know that the more the world mass media use harsh words and the more the Western and Eastern satanic powers oppress the people of the world, is a proof of their Divine Power and Almighty God will remunerate them for their acts here and in the Hereafter. *"Truly, He is the Benefactor of all blessings and in His hand lies the dominion over all things."* [1]

I humbly and earnestly advise the Muslim community to follow the Infallible Imams and the political, social, economic and military teachings and culture of these great guides to humanity with devotion, sincerity and sacrifice. I would like to enjoin all of you to safeguard and observe the *Fiqh-e-Sunnati*[2] (traditional jurisprudence) or religious canons. These set forth the schools of Prophetic mission and Imamate and guarantee the growth and development of the nations through their primary and secondary decrees, [3] both of which are the schools of Islamic jurisprudence. My advice is that they should not deviate an iota from the teachings of both schools of Islamic jurisprudence and not listen to the whisperings of the slinking devils, who are the enemies of religion and truth. They should know that the slightest deviation is the beginning of the downfall of the religion, rules of Islam, and the Divine Government of Justice. They should never neglect Friday prayer [4]

---

[1] The Holy Quran (23:88).

[2] The term *'fiqh'* was defined earlier. *'Sunnati'* is a method transmitted to us by the ancients. With this explanation, the *Fiqh-e-Sunnati* or Traditional Jurisprudence is a method for deducing and extracting religious rules and decrees from authentic and reliable sources, a procedure pursued by the learned authorities of the Shiah denomination from the earliest days of the Infallible Imams to the present; they accept no alternative to it.

[3] The Book and the Tradition embody many of the laws or precepts concerning social relations needed by the Muslims and their decrees are specified in whole or in part. This group of commands are known as 'primary decrees'. However, in the administration of the society, the Islamic government occasionally faces issues and problems for which primary decrees do not point to a solution. In instances like this, Islam has empowered the governor to use his sovereign right of *wilayat* or guardianship and, by considering the interests of the society, legislate a set of rules and regulations and thereby solve those difficulties. This type of laws are counted as 'secondary decrees'.

[4] Friday *Namaz* or prayer is one of the Islam's major act of worship and social rituals. It is performed every Friday in congregation by believers. Prior to the start of *namaz*, the leader of the mass performs two sermons during which he acquaints the Muslims with their individual and social duties and keeps them abreast of the current problems of the country, the world and Islamic issues. Friday Prayer is a tradition of the Prophet (*s*) and the Infallible Imams (pbut). It is so important that even prison inmates must participate in it. In the course of Islamic history, nothing has been as effective as Friday Prayer in unifying the people, imparting information to them and making them alert.

and daily congregational prayer,[1] which exhibit the political aspect of prayer. Indeed, they must never neglect Friday prayer, one of the greatest blessings of Allah, the Exalted, which is best performed in the Islamic Republic of Iran. They should also not neglect the mourning ceremonies for the Infallible Imams, especially for the leader of the oppressed and the most prestigious of the martyrs, His Holiness Imam Husayn;[2] May the Peace and Blessings of Allah, His Prophet, His Angels and the righteous be upon his great and brave soul! They should know whatever decrees there are from the Infallible Imams about honoring the mourning ceremony regarding historical martyrdom of Imam Husayn (s) and whatever maledictions and curses there are on those who transgressed against the *Ahl al-Bayt*[3] (the progeny of the

---

[1] In the Divine disciplines of the Prophet, *namaz* or *salat* prayer is the ascension of the terrestrial men to the highest moral stature and a means for approach to the Creator of the world, He who prevents man's depravity and mental pollution. On the other hand, *namaz* or *salat*, if said in congregation with its particular characteristics, develops an ideal society and purges human societies of pollution and rust. It is by means of this support that the Islamic government can approach its goals and achieve unity which is one of the Divine covenants of the Prophets (s) and is emphatically recommended by the Infallible Imams (pbut). Therefore, saying *namaz* in congregation is confirmed and emphasized by the great authorities of Islam.

[2] Hussein (s) was the hero of Ashura, the greatest epic event in man's history, which happened on the 10th day of Muharram when Imam Hussein (s) was martyred. He was born to Ali (s), the man of justice and chastity and Her Holiness Fatimah (s), the symbol of a Muslim woman, in the 4th year A.H. After the martyrdom of Imam Hasan (s) in 50 A.H., Muaviyeh the Caliph increased his pressure and ordered all his governors to delete the names of the Shiite Muslims (followers of Ali—s)—from the rosters of the Muslim treasury, to apprehend and put to death any one accused of sympathy with Ali (s). Yazid succeeded his father Muaviyeh as a caliph and followed the path of his sire. He suggested that Imam Hussein swear allegiance to him or be slain should he refuse.

Imam Hussein did not yield to Yazid, this prototype of meanness and villainy. Imam resorted to the sword and undertook the fundamental Ashura move so that he might thus kindle a light of hope amid the darkness of oppression and initiating history's eternal epic event. By sacrificing his life and the lives of his kins and followers in the Path of Allah, Imam Hussein (s) became a model and an example for all his followers in the path of Allah; Imam Hussein (s) became a model and an example for all those who died in the path of Truth. Many books have been written about the personality of Imam Husayn (s) and a great deal has been talked about him. Friend and foes testify to Imam Husayn's matchless courage, patience, fight against cruelty and injustice, courtesy and humbleness, kindness and compassion.

[3] In common usage, the term ahl-ul-beyt' refers to those who live in a man's house and all together make up his household including wife, sons and daughters. Unimpeachable narratives, recorded and quoted in both Sunnite and Shiite books and other reliable sources, indicate that the term ahl-ol-beyt' is a 'blessing' that applies to the family of the Prophet (s), Ali (s), Fatimah (s), Hasan (s) and Husayn (s) exclusively. However, according to these narratives and others, nine other Infallible Imams who are of Imam Husayn's progeny are included in the ahl al-Bayt or household. The Holy Quran recommends love for the *Ahl al-*

Prophet—s) are the same cries of protest of the oppressed against criminal leaders throughout history until the end of time. You should know that maledictions, curses and cries of protest against the oppressions of Bani Ummayeh,[1] Allah's curse be upon them, though they have already been perished and gone to the Hell, also reflect the cries of protest by the oppressed against the oppressors of the world. It is the perpetuation of such cries of protest that shatters oppression.

It is necessary that the crimes of the tyrants in each age and era be regularly condemned in the cries of lamentations and in the recitals of elegies held for the Infallible Imams. In this age which is the age of oppression of the world of Islam by America and Russia and their satellites, including the Saudi family these traitors to the great Divine sanctuary, His Prophet and His Angels—the crimes of these oppressors must be strikingly reminded, cursed and imprecated. We all should know that it is these politico-religious ceremonies that give Muslims, particularly the Shiite Muslims, (these followers of the Infallible Imams), the unity they should enjoy; these also preserve the nationality of all Muslims.

This politico-religious testament of mine is not intended for the great nation of Iran only. Rather, it is recommended to all Islamic nations and the oppressed peoples of the world regardless of their religion or nationality.

I humbly pray the Almighty God not to leave us and our nations to ourselves even for a moment. May He not withhold His blessings from the children of Islam and the cherished Muslim combatants.

Ruhullah al-Musawi al-Khomeini

In the Name of God, the Compassionate, the Merciful

The glorious Islamic Revolution of Iran, which is the product of efforts of millions of valuable human beings, thousands of martyrs and disabled of the war—these living martyrs—is the source of hope for millions of Muslims and the oppressed people throughout the world. It is so great that its

---

Bayt or the Prophet's Household by the Muslim community. Such love is deemed as the reward of the Prophet (*s*).

[1] Muawiyah, son of Abusufyan and the grandson of Ummayah declared himself the Caliph of Muslims in 41 A.H. (661 A.D.) just after His Holiness Imam Ali (*s*) was martyred. The Ummayeh clan held the caliphate until 132 A.H. (720 A.D.) The Ummayeh rulers revived aristocracy and the hereditary monarchy which is in sharp conflict with basic Islamic faith. History is replete with accounts of painful events in the Islamic world during the Ummayeh rule, events like ruthless massacre, imprisonment and banishment of the Household of the Prophet (*s*), martyrdom of Imam Husayn (*s*) by agents of Yazid (son of Muawiyah), etc.

assessment is beyond written prose and expression. I, Ruhullah Musawi Khomeini, despite all my shortcomings, do not give up hope in the great generosity of Allah, the most Exalted. The sustenance of my perilous path to the Hereafter is my hope in the generosity of the Absolute Benefactor. As a humble student of theology, like other Muslim brothers, I have hope in this revolution, perpetuation of its outcome and its increasing fruition. I would like to express some matters to the beloved present and future generations. Even though they may sound repetitious, I beg the Forgiving Allah to bless my remarks.

1. We know that this great revolution, which has virtually cut off the hands of the world aggressors and oppressors from Iran, succeeded only with Unseen Divine blessings; otherwise, it would have been impossible for a nation of 36 million to succeed despite all the anti-Islamic and anti-clerical propaganda, especially in the last century. The revolution triumphed despite immeasurable discord triggered by international writers and orators in the media and through speeches, meetings, gatherings, poems, anecdotes and jokes in circles indulged in immorality, debauchery, gambling, drugs and alcohol. All of these were used to lead the younger generation, who should have been active for the progress and excellence of their beloved country, to corruption and to indifference towards evil deeds of the corrupt Shah and his ignoramus father, puppet governments and parliaments imposed upon our nation through the embassies of the powerful foreign governments. The most flagrant was the condition of the universities, high schools and educational centers, on which the future of the country depends. These centers employed teachers and professors who were fascinated with the West or the East and were absolutely opposed to Islamic culture and to patriotic values. Among these teachers and professors were, of course, some committed and considerate ones. However, they were too few and too restricted to take appropriate action. Along with these and tens of other problems, including exile and isolation of the clerics and defaming many of them through malicious propaganda, it would have been impossible for this nation to revolt unitedly throughout the country. They were not unified in target with the motto of *Allahu Akbar* and with dazzling and miraculous sacrifices to drive away all the internal and external powers and to take the reins of power into their own hands. Therefore, the Islamic Revolution in Iran is totally different from all other revolutions. The inception, the nature of the struggle and the incentive for 'Revolution' were all different. There is no doubt that it was a

Divine gift and blessing from the Unseen granted by Allah the Almighty to this oppressed and pillaged nation.

2. Islam or Islamic government is a Divine phenomenon the implementation of which, guarantees the happiness of its followers in this world and the Hereafter in the best possible way and has the potential to eliminate tyranny, corruption and transgression, and leading humankind to its ultimate desired goal. It is a school of thought that, unlike polytheistic schools, carefully intervenes and supervises individual, social, material, spiritual, cultural, political, military and economic aspects of life and does not neglect any point which may have a bearing on the growth of man and society as well as their material and spiritual progress. It warns people of all difficulties and obstacles standing on the way of perfection in order to eradicate them. Now that, with the blessed support of Allah and with the endeavor of the committed nation the foundation of the Islamic Republic has been laid, we should bear in mind that what is important in establishing the Islamic government is Islam itself and its progressive rules. It is formidable for the great nation of Iran to ensure the implementation and protection of Islamic values in all aspects of life. The safeguard Islam itself is the most important obligations. All Great Prophets from His Holiness Adam (*s*) to His Holiness Muhammad (*s*) have strived and sacrificed for the protection of the concept of Islam;[1] no deterrent ever stopped them from fulfilling this great obligation. After the Prophets, their committed followers and the Infallible Imams (*s*) strove for the protection of Islam to the point of sacrificing their holy blood. Today, it is an obligation for the Iranian nation, in particular, and the Muslim community, in general, to protect ardently this Divine trust, which has been officially established in Iran and which has already generated an outstanding outcome in such a short time. They must struggle to provide the means for its perpetuation and for removal of all obstacles. It is hoped that the reflection of its light shall reach all Islamic communities and lead governments and nations to obtain an understanding of this vital issue in order to curb the grip of world-devouring superpowers, the worst criminals in the history of mankind, from the oppressed people of the world.

Knowing that I am approaching my last breath of life, I deem it my duty to address the present and future generations and explain what could affect the protection and perpetuation of this Divine trust, warning against the perils and hindrances posing a threat to the revolution. I beg the Creator, the Sustainer of the universe to grant prosperity and felicity to all.

---

[1] Islam as a concept means total submission to Almighty God.

A. The secret of the perpetuation of the Islamic Revolution is undoubtedly the same that led the revolution to its success. This is known to the nation today; the future generations would learn through history that its two essential foundations are: a) Divine incentive to establish the Islamic government and b) solidarity of people all over the country struggling for the same incentive and aspiration with one voice.

I advise all present and future generations that if you want Islam and Allah's sovereignty to prevail and if you want the influence of superpowers and external and internal exploiters to be curtailed over your countries, do not lose the Divine incentive the Almighty God has revealed in the Glorious Quran. That which defies this incentive which is the secret of success, is to neglect the prime aspiration that would eventually result in disunity and discord. This is why the trumpets of propaganda are sounding off everywhere. Local agents are spending millions of dollars on sowing the seeds of discord for distortion of facts by spreading rumors and lies. Frequent visits of the enemies of the Islamic Republic to our region prove their malicious motivations. Unfortunately, among them are the leaders of some Islamic states who think of nothing except their own personal interests and who have been totally submitted to the will of USA. Some pseudo-clerics have also joined the 'club'.

What is important for the Iranian people and the Muslims of the world today and in the future is to challenge these divisive and destructive propaganda. My recommendation to Muslims, especially to Iranians in the present age, is to defy strongly these conspiracies and consolidate their unity in any possible way in order to disappoint the *Kuffar*[1] and *Munafiqin*.[2]

B. One of the most important conspiracies against Islam, being clearly observed in the present century, particularly in recent decades and after the success of the Islamic Revolution, is the vast and multidimensional propaganda aimed at discouraging nations, particularly the devoted people of Iran. Sometimes they adduce the clumsy argument that the modern world cannot be administered by laws established 1400 years ago. They naively argue that Islam is a retrogressive religion opposed to innovation or manifestation of modern civilization. They claim that it is not becoming of a country to be isolated from the modern progressive world. At other times, they claim that Islam and other Divine religions simply deal with spiritual

---

[1] Unbelievers.
[2] Hypocrites.

matters and purification of the soul, rejecting worldly affairs. Cunningly and shrewdly, they pretend to be defending the sanctities of Islam, arguing that acts of worship, remembrance of God and supplication bring man closer to Almighty God, but keep man away from material life. They further argue that being involved in governmental politics and political affairs defies all those great ideals and sublime spiritual objectives, arriving at the conclusion that all this is to make man's material life better and is, therefore, against the principles of the Great Prophets. Unfortunately, this latter argument has influenced some of the clerics and religious people being informed of Islam to the degree that they consider—and perhaps some still do—that participation in governmental and political affairs is sinful and corruptive. This was a tragedy, which had befallen Islam.

The proponents of the first argument are either incognizant or intentionally act as if they were incognizant about government, law and politics, because many are the concepts that are not liable to passage of time. Implementing law based on equity and justice, opposing tyrannical and oppressive governments, establishing individual and social justice, suppressing corruption and immorality, spreading liberty based on intellect, justice and independence; fighting against colonization, exploitation and dictatorship, observance of *Hudud*,[1] *Qisas*[2] and *Tazirat*[3] based on justified criteria to protect communities against immorality; governing and ruling nations based on intellect, justice and fairness and hundreds of similar questions are not things that could become outdated in the course of history or man's life. It is absurd to say that social justice, which was to be practiced from the beginning of creation and fighting against crimes and cruelties, which were to be avoided, can no longer be exercised in the age of atom. The claim that Islam is against modern innovations—like the same claim made by the deposed Muhammad Rida Pahlavi to the effect that "These people (Islamic Revolutionaries) want to travel with four-legged animals"—is nothing but an idiotic accusation. If innovation and new features of civilization mean inventions, new scientific discoveries and industrial progress, it should be known that neither Islam nor any other monotheistic religion has ever opposed such things. On the contrary, Islam and the Holy Quran emphatically cultivate scientific and industrial development. If, however, 'civilization' and 'modernization' are what is implied by some professional intellectuals, i.e. freedom to indulge in all sorts of immoral and

---

[1] In Islamic law, a fixed punishment for committing acts of immorality and transgression.
[2] A punishment determined by Islamic court.
[3] In Islamic law, it means a punishment against criminals and assailants.

perverse acts, including even homosexuality, then all Divine religions, noble scholars and wise men of reason are opposed to them, even though some pro-Eastern or pro-Western individuals promote these ideas blindly.

The second category of the adversaries of Islam, who entertain more vicious plots, suggest that religion and politics are incompatible and should not be integrated. These ignorant individuals should be informed that the Glorious Quran and the Tradition of the Prophet of Islam (s) accommodate more rules and decrees regarding government and politics than any other subject. In fact, a great deal of Islamic laws concerning worship such as Congregational and Friday Prayer have political aspects as well. Neglecting such politico-religious ceremonies has led to many disadvantages. The Prophet of Islam (s) founded a government just like any other governments but with the spirit and motivation of promoting social justice, equity, and human rights. The early caliphs of Islam ruled extensive governments. The history of Islam clearly reveals that the government of Ali Bin Abitalib (s) had even a broader and more extensive dimension to institute his administration. Unfortunately, most of the later Islamic governments were only nominals. Even now there are plenty who claim that they are running Islamic governments and following Islam and the Holy Prophet (s).

In this final will and testament, I briefly mention these points in passing and hope that writers, sociologists and historians can elaborate on the ideas, which have influenced the Muslim nations wrongly. This conviction that the prophets and Islam are only concerned with spiritual and moral issues and that governments are only concerned with secular or temporal matters are totally wrong. What must be opposed are satanic governments, dictatorial rules, injustice, thirst for power, greed for wealth and, finally worldly matters that would make a human being neglect Almighty God. This is what all the Prophets of Allah (pbut) and the Infallible Imams (pbut) have repeatedly warned against. The Divine rule that is for the benefit of the dispossessed and the oppressed and that seeks to prevent cruelty and injustice is exactly what Sulayman Bin Dawud and the Great Prophet of Islam (s) tried to establish. This is one of the greatest Divine duties and ranks among the highest acts of worship same as the sound and healthy politics which existed in the above-mentioned governments and is among the essentials. The alert nation of Iran must, frustrate these conspiracies with an Islamic insight. Committed writers and preachers must rise up to help the nation to stop the plotting devils.

C. Of the same sort of conspiracies, if not more insidious, are the widespread rumors throughout the country, such as: "Islamic Republic has done nothing for the people of Iran. These innocent people made sacrifices with great zeal and enthusiasm to remove the oppressive regime of the *Taghut* but became captives of a worse regime. The transgressors have become more transgressive and the oppressed more oppressed. Prisons are filled with the youth who are the hope of the future. Torture is more inhumane and severe than before. Everyday a number of men are executed in the name of Islam. If only it was not called 'The Islamic Republic'. Today is worse than the time of Reza Khan and his son. People are suffering from hardship. Inflation is driving people mad. The authorities are leading this regime toward communism. People's properties are being confiscated. Freedom is totally spared from the people and so forth." Such rumors are proofs of planned conspiracies that are carried out daily in different forms, in different towns and boroughs, in taxi cabs, in buses, at small gatherings, and so on. As soon as one false rumor wears off, a fresh one takes its place. Unfortunately, even some simple-minded clerics unaware of the satanic tricks believe in such baseless rumors being contacted with a few agents behind the conspiracy. The fact is that many of those, who listen to the rumors and accept them, are persons lacking knowledge of the world conditions, of world revolutions, and of post-revolutionary events and their inevitable aftermath. They lack knowledge of the events that have occurred in favor of Islamic values. They hear such rumors and accept them blindly and naively either deliberately or delinquently.

My humble request to everyone remains, not to criticize the present situation before studying the present world condition and comparing the Islamic Revolution of Iran with other revolutions. Do not find fault before becoming familiar with the predicament of other revolutionary countries and nations during and after their revolutions. Before any criticism you should probe into the sufferings of this country pillaged by the *Taghuti* actions of Reza Khan and his son Muhammad Reza. His pillaging has entangled the present government with many problems to resolve. These problems range from disastrous dependencies all the way to the ill-managed ministries, governmental offices, the economy and the armed forces. Centers of debauchery and liquor stores were on the increase. Permissiveness in all walks of life, education in high schools and universities and conditions of the cabarets and brothel houses, the youth, clerics and religious people, committed freedom-seekers and virtuous oppressed young women and mosques during the *Taghut* rule are part of predicament. Inquire into the files of those who were executed and imprisoned and inspect the conditions of prisons and the persons in charge of them. Investigate into the wealth of the wealthy people, large land-grabbers and hoarders of products and trade monopolists and speculators. Compare the conditions of the courts of justice and the judges in pre-and post-Revolution. Appraise the personality of the representatives of the Islamic parliament, members of the government, provincial governors and other public officials. Investigate into the performance of the government and works of the Reconstruction Jihad [1] in poor villages, where are deprived even from drinking water and hospitals. Consider the consequences of the imposed war, such as accommodation of several millions of Afghani and Iraqi refugees. Take into account handling and supporting the disabled and the martyrs' families, not to mention the imposed economic sanctions against Iran and conspiracies by America and her international and local agents. Add to the above-mentioned problems, lack of well-trained Islamic missionary to propagate true Islamic values as well as low number of qualified religious judges, the chaos raised by the corrupt enemies of Islam and the revolution plus ignorant friends and tens of other difficulties. My request again is that, before you have become familiar enough with these problems, avoid nitpicking and engaging in destructive and poisonous criticism. Think considerately of this lonely present day and Islam how it was left alone during centuries of rule of oppressive rulers along with the ignorance of the masses and its newly born infant, i.e. the Islamic Revolution, which is threatened by external and internal enemies. You, the fault-finders, should question yourselves. Is it not better to try to correct the situation instead of making harsh criticisms instead of defending the hypocrites, oppressors, owners of wealth and trade monopolists who lack divine consciousness, would it not be better to defend the oppressed and the deprived people? Furthermore, ask yourselves if it is not better to try to take into consideration either the martyred clerics or the devoted officials instead of indirectly defending rebellions?

    I have never claimed, and will never do, that Islamic laws have been fully implemented after the revolution. I do not say that some personalities do not violate Islamic rules due to ignorance or certain complexes. But I do say that the legislative, judicial and executive branches of the government are trying their best to Islamize this country with the support of the entire nation. So much the better if these minority groups introspect and wake up to the

---

[1] Performing *Jihad* in the path of Allah is one of the most important duties of every Muslim. In 1980, Imam Khomeini (*s*) asked the people to participate in the Reconstruction Movement. Thus a revolutionary institution called 'the Reconstruction Jihad' was formed that began to operate on a voluntary basis. This was later expanded into a ministry known as 'the Ministry of *Jihad*.

reality. Even if they do not join the awakened mass, still Islamic and humanistic ideals would be actualized as our masses of people are informed, alert and considerate. Deviant groups shall be defeated by the roaring tide of the mass.

I am highly convinced that today the Iranian nation enjoy greater integrity than the people of Hijaz at the time of the prophet (*s*) and the people of Iraq and Kufah at the time of Imam Ali (*s*) and Imam Husayn (*s*). When the holy prophet Muhammad (*s*) was still alive, people of Hijaz disobeyed him and feigned excuses for not going to war fronts. For this, Almighty God has rebuked them severely in *Surah Al-Baraah* of the Glorious Quran. So much, they accused the prophet (*s*) of lying and the holy prophet cursed them for such as accusation on the pulpit. Imam Ali's (*s*) complaints against mistreatments and disobedience of the people of Kufah have provided food for many books of tradition and history. Disobedience and infidelity of the people of Iraq and Kufeh toward Imam Husayn (*s*) resulted in history's greatest tragic epic event, i.e. martyrdom of Imam Husayn (*a*). Those who did not participate in the act of martyrdom either fled or sat idly. They watched that historic crime taking place. But today, we observe how the Iranian nation wholeheartedly supports its armed forces, the police, *Sepah*,[1] *Basij*,[2] and tribal volunteers making unthinkable sacrifices at the war fronts and behind the front lines. We are delighted at the invaluable assistance by people all over the country. We are proud to see the families of our martyrs and the disabled war veterans and their kins meet all of us with open arms and displaying such reassuring reactions and words. All this is due to their deep faith in Almighty God and their love for Him, Islam and the Hereafter. All these are taking place at a time when they are neither in the company of the prophet (*s*) nor an Infallible Imam (*s*). They are purely motivated by their belief and certainty in the Unseen. This is the divine mystery behind the victory in various aspects. Islam is proud of training such children. We are all honored to live in this age and in the presence of such nation.

Here, I advise those who oppose the Islamic Republic with any incentive and those boys or girls, who have been misled by *Munafiqin*[3] and

---

[1] The Islamic Revolution Guard corps.
[2] A volunteer group besieged to defend the revolution and to render nationwide services to maintain Islamic values. This group came into existence in 1979 following the order of Imam Khomeini.
[3] Literally, it means hypocrites. In this context, it means the partisan fighter group called '*Mujahidin*' that was formed in 1965 to challenge the Shah. But after the victory of the Islamic Revolution, a group under the same title took a position against the revolution; they martyred a

opportunists, to pass judgments objectively and open-mindedly. I advise them to examine the content of the propaganda put out by those who wish to see the fall of the Islamic Republic. They should carefully watch the enemies' behavior towards the deprived masses, and the support they receive from foreign agents, the suspicious groups, and individuals who have joined them, their unethical communal code of practice and behavior, and the treacherous shifting of their stance in confronting different situations. They should study the character of those martyred in this Islamic Republic by *Munafiqin* and the corrupt people. They should evaluate and compare the martyrs with those who martyred them. Recorded cassettes and video tapes of both groups are available for ultimate judgment to see which group is the defender of the deprived and the oppressed people.

You will not read these pages before my death. You will read them after my death, when I am no longer among you. Then you cannot accuse me speaking for my self-interests or convincing you to acquire certain position or power or influencing your minds and hearts. Since you are a worthy generation, I wish you to spend your young days in the way of Allah, the beloved Islam and the Islamic Republic in order to earn prosperity in this world and the Hereafter. I beg the Forgiving Allah to guide you to the straight path of humanity and to forgive our sins through His Expansive Mercy. You too, in your own privacy, beg the same thing from Allah because He is the Guide and the Compassionate.

I also extend my advice to the noble people of Iran as well as other nations who are suffering under corrupt governments that are at the service of the superpowers. I specifically address you, the beloved people of Iran, to protect and guard the blessings of this revolution, which you have earned with your great holy war and with the blood of your brave children and dear ones. Cherish it as the most precious thing to you. Guard and preserve it as a supreme divine blessing of Allah. Do not fear the difficulties, which will appear on this straight path because: *"If you assist the religion of Allah, He will assist you and will make your steps steadfast"*.[1] Take part wholeheartedly and sincerely in resolving the problems of the Islamic Republic. Consider yourselves as part of the government and the parliament and safeguard them as precious belongings.

I also advise the parliament, the government and the authorities to appreciate the people of this country and serve them well, particularly the

---

large number of government officials and true believers of the Islamic Revolution. This is why the nation called them "*Munafiqin*", meaning hypocrites.

[1] The Holy Quran (47:7).

oppressed and the deprived who are the light of our eyes and whose sacrifices made the formation of the Islamic Republic possible, perpetuation of which is due to their devotion. The authorities should regard themselves attached to the people and recognize them as part of their own being. They are also recommended to condemn the *Taghuti* governments constantly, a band of notorious plunderers and empty-headed bullies, of course in a manner which is becoming an Islamic government.

I advise the Muslim nations to consider the government of the Islamic Republic and the crusading people of Iran as an ideal example and to resist their oppressive governments strongly, since they do not submit to the will of their nations. They should remember that the cause of plight of Muslims are the governments which depend on the East or the West. I emphatically recommend these nations, not to pay attention to the sirens of antagonisitic propaganda against Islam and the Islamic Republic sounded by those who cunningly attempt to force Islam to the sidelines in order to foster the interests of the superpowers.

D. Isolating the clerics is a satanic plot of colonialists and exploiters and has been employed for a long time. In Iran, this plot gained momentum during the reign of Reza Khan and continued up to the time of Muhammad Reza. Reza Khan pursued the conspiracy using several methods such as: persecution, forcing the clerics to abandon their clerical robes, imprisonment, exile, insulation, execution, and so on. Muhammad Reza employed different approach such as creating animosity between university professors and clerics employing a great deal of propaganda. Unfortunately, due to the fact that both groups were unaware of the satanic conspiracy of the superpowers, grave consequences were deduced as it was planned. Efforts were made to choose teachers, professors and presidents of high schools and universities from among those who were fascinated by the West or the East and those deviated from Islam and other religions in order to leave the committed believers in minority. So that the would-be-managers who are expected to run the government in future would be brought up from the very childhood in such a manner that they would detest all religions in general, Islam in particular, and the religious propagators, especially the Muslim clerics. Muslim clerics were accused of being British agents at that time and later on (at the time of Muhammad Rida) were accused of being supporters of capitalists, land mongers, and reactionaries opposed to civilization and progress. On the other hand, through malicious propaganda, they created doubts among the clerics towards the university scholars as well as students, accusing them of secularism, recklessness, and opposition to all aspects of Islam and other religions. The results were that government officials would become anti-religion, anti-Islam, and anti-cleric, thus the masses of people who loved the religion and the clerics would become anti-government and whatever related to it. The deep gap between government and the nation, and between the university and the clerics opened the way to the exploiters and the plunderers so much so that the fate of the people and all the resources of the country fell into their hands and pockets and the nation suffered as we all witnessed.

Now, by Allah's will and sacrifices of the entire nation including clerics, university people, businessmen, people of bazaar, workers, agricultural and industrial workers and other segments, fetters of bondage have been removed and chains of enslavement broken. Arrogant powers have been repelled and the country saved from their clutches of these powers and their domestic puppets. I would like to advise the present and future generations "not to slacken their efforts". Let the university professors and students strengthen their bonds of friendship and mutual understanding with the clerics and the students of theology. They should never underestimate the plots of the cunning enemy. Whenever they see someone trying to sow the seeds of discord, they should provide counsel and guidance for them. If their advice to such individuals is not effective, they should turn away from them, isolate them and not let their conspiracies take root, for "prevention is better than cure". If, among the professors, there is someone who tries to mislead the students by distorting the truth, they should guide him; if he keeps up with causing deviation, they should reject him by boycotting his classes. This duty is mainly directed towards the honorable clerics and the religious students. Altogether conspiracies have a special trend in the universities. The alert individuals and students must react wisely and promptly to all sorts of conspiracies.

E. One of the most effective conspiracies that has unfortunately left an undeniable mark on the nations, including ours, is the alienation of the people of colonized countries with their own cultures. In other words, 'Westernized' or 'Easternized' intellectuals became alienated with their own cultures; they came to regard the people related to the superpowers as having superior culture and race compared to that of their own. They looked upon the superpowers as their *Qiblah*[1] and thought that affiliation with either of the

---

[1] It is the Ka'ba in Mecca, the direction to which Muslims face when saying daily prayers.

two power poles is an inevitable issue. This sad story has a lengthy background. The blows we have received, and are still receiving, are seriously devastating and fatal.

Another unhappy and mischievous plot woven by the superpowers is to prevent the oppressed and colonized nations from progression and to keep them backward in order to make them consumers rather than producers. The imperialistic powers have so frightened us through their satanic might that we dare not venture into any initiatives. Rather we have submitted our minds and fates to them and became their followers with closed eyes and ears. This shallowness and state of feeling absurd has resulted in losing our self-reliance and power of initiation, thus blindly imitating the West and the East in every aspect. Whatever heritage we possessed whether cultural, scientific or industrial was belittled, criticized and ridiculed by ignorant writers and lecturers bewitched by the West or the East that constantly suppressed and frustrated our own native potentiality. They promoted foreign culture and imposed it on us. No matter how vulgar, shameful and degrading, the propagate it. For instance, if books contain a number of foreign words and terms, they are accepted right away with respect irrespective of their meanings. Their authors and speakers are regarded as scholars and bright individuals. If whatever and wherever we look at from cradle to grave has a Western or Eastern label, it is favored and valued, being considered as a sign of progress and civilization. If anything has a domestic and traditional label, it is rejected and considered as outdated, backward and useless. Choosing foreign names for our children is regarded as a prestigious matter, whereas choosing traditional names is considered as fanaticism and backwardness. Streets, avenues, stores, companies, drugstores, libraries and even local products must bear foreign names in order to be attractive and acceptable to people. Imitating western mannerism in all walks of life and in all aspects of social association is regarded as a token of honor, civilization and progress. On the contrary, traditional modes of conduct and customs are deemed as retrograde and ancestor-praising. Going abroad for treatment even for minor ailments that are easily cured at home is the thing to do, thus causing disappointment and degradation for our well-qualified physicians. Making a trip to England, France, U.S.A., or Moscow enhances one's dignity while paying pilgrimage to Mecca or visiting other holy shrines and blessed places is considered sign of being backward and old-fashioned. Overlooking whatever related to religion, rituals and spirituality is a sign of open-mindedness and civilization whereas commitment to these issues a sign of being backward and old-fashioned.

I do not say that we have everything. It is a fact that in the course of recent history, especially during the last decades, we have been deprived of any progress. The treacherous statesmen of the Pahlavi regime and their propaganda belittled every domestic product and created inferiority complexes in us, thus depriving us from achieving any advancement. Importation of all types of goods from abroad, particularly entertainment and luxurious commodities such as cosmetics and childish games, which provided channels for our young men and women, and mainly the youth, was meant to make them preoccupied with such trivial things and cause them to be consumers of such things as well as items of luxury which has a long and sad story. No effort was spared in diverting the attention of our youth, as most dynamic members of the society, to establishing centers of debauchery and pleasure-seeking. Tens of these malicious plots are all conceived only for the purpose of keeping countries like ours backward. Now that the Iranian nation is, to a large extent, freed from such traps and the deprived generation has risen to create and construct at its own initiatives, commodities, many examples of which we are witnessing, such as aircraft spare parts, that were thought could not be provided locally and our hands were extended to the West or the East for manufacturing such items. This is because economic blockade and the compelling conditions of the imposed war [1] made their domestic production without assistance of foreign experts possible. Such items were produced more economically and they satisfied our needs. Our people have proved to be able to do things if they want.

I humbly recommend our people to be alert and watchful and do not let the West-or East-affiliated politicians draw us back towards the international plunderers. Take decisive actions to do away with all dependencies.

Be sure that the Aryan or Arab races are in no way less graded than the European, American or Russian races. If you succeed in finding your true selves and do not let despair overtake you and rely on yourselves and expect nothing of others, you shall be able to do and make everything in the long run. This is possible provided that you rely on Almighty God, earn self-

---

[1] Because of the victory of the Islamic Revolution in Iran, the U.S.A. lost one of the most sensitive strategic areas of the world and its access to the immense oil reserves was cut off. Therefore, by hook or by crook, America tried to restore its losses. Actions taken by the U.S.A. in this connection include: aid to domestic insurgents, military attack on Iran (known as Tabas incursion) and masterminding a coup d'etat. As none of these were effective, America tried something else; it made the adventurous Iraqi regime to impose an undeclared war on the Islamic Revolution. The cost several hundred thousand of human lives; hundreds of thousands men maimed, wounded or taken captive. The superpowers and their bonded servant Saddam Hussein (president of Iraq) could not achieve any one of their objectives.

reliance and cut off all ties of dependencies on others. Moreover, you should endure hardship in order to achieve an honorable state of life and attain liberation from the influence and domination of others.

It is incumbent on the authorities both in the present and the future governments to cherish and appreciate their experts and specialists and encourage them through moral and material support to take initiatives. The government and political leaders should not allow import of goods that encourage consumerism and destroy domestic economy. Let the people be content with whatever they have until they can make everything themselves.

I ask the youth, boys and girls not to compromise their freedom, independence and human values for luxury, pleasure-seeking and other vices that are offered to them by the corrupt agents of the West or the East. Experience has taught us that these affiliated puppets think of nothing except degenerating the youth and making them feel indifferent towards their own destinies and that of their country. The agents are engaged in plundering our natural resources and expanding the level of consumerism among people. In short, they work to pave the way for colonization and exploitation. For all these reasons, they try to keep a highly civilized nation such as ours in a state of backwardness, underdevelopment, and semi-primitive conditions.

F. One of their major plots mentioned earlier, is to take over the educational centers, especially the universities whose trained output would naturally take the control of the country in their hands. Their methods with respect to the clerics and the schools of Islamic sciences is different from that of the universities and high schools. Their plot is to remove the clerics from the scene and to isolate them. During the time of Reza Khan, a great deal of torture and persecution were used to achieve this purpose, but, thank God, the result was reversed. With propaganda, false accusations and devilish plans, they tried to segregate the educated and the so-called intellectuals. This continued during the time of Muhammad Reza cunningly and without apparent violence.

As to university, their plan is to alienate the youth with their own values and cultural identity in order to draw them over to the East or the West and to select the statesmen from among them. These selected individuals were instituted in positions of authority and doing whatever they want to the country. They plundered the country's resources and exploited the people through their internal agents. Nevertheless, the clerics, who had been isolated, despised and defeated, reacted passively to the case. This is the best way to hold a nation in a backward state and to plunder the countries under their domination. It is easy for superpowers and of no cost to them while the whole wealth of nations goes to their pockets smoothly.

Now that due to 'the revolution' we are involved in the act of purging the universities and teacher-training colleges, it is necessary for all of us to help the officials and not ever let these institutions deviate from the right path. Take the necessary action as soon as you notice any deviation. This vital task should be primarily carried out by universities students. To save the university from deviation and perversion is to save the nation and the country.

I hereby urge our youth, their parents and friends as well as statesmen and intellectuals who care for the country to participate in this important task wholeheartedly to maintain the safety of the country and to deliver purified universities to the next generation. I also advice coming generations to guard the universities against tendency to the West or the East, as this is necessary for salvation of themselves, the country and beloved Islam. This humane and Islamic act cuts off the hands of superpowers from the country and makes them lose all hope. May Allah bless and protect you!

G. Commitment of the representatives of the Islamic Consultative Assembly is a major issue. We witnessed the damage that Islam and Iran suffered at the hands of the corrupt and perverted representatives of the former parliament since the constitutional regime [1] was initiated in the country through the era of the Pahlavi dynasty. Such parliament representatives were worthless individuals, servants of foreign powers; they betrayed the country and the nation. During the fifty years of the tyrannical rule of the Pahlavi regime, a majority of sham parliament representatives was forged, carrying out the dictates of the Soviet Union, England and America

---

[1] By the end of 19th-and early 20th-centuries, the Iranian people had become obsessed with the cruelty and injustice of the rulers and agents of despotism and dictatorship as well as with chaotic conditions of the country and the atrocities of the government agents.

Weakness and incompetence of Muzaffaruddin Shah, the monarch of the time, in administering the affairs of the state and the increasing awakening of the people and other factors, like the rise of the clerics and religious authorities, provided grounds for a revolution known as the 'Constitutional Movement,' which triumphed in 6091after long and hard struggle.

Though not led in the right channel, the movement effected great changes in the social structure of Iran, breakdown of class distinction, upsetting the power position of the courtiers, the big landlords and the institution of law and justice. However, the Constitutional Movement failed to yield the desired results because of the influence of pro-West elements and removal of the clerics from politics and government rule; hereditary monarchy was reinstituted with a coup d'etat by Rida Khan.

in order to exploit the country and the nation. After the constitution was initiated in Iran, its major articles were almost always ignored. Before Reza Khan came to power, the country was in the hands of a number of treacherous pro-West feudal overlords. Then came the tyrant Pahlavi regime and its cruel agents.

Now that by the Grace of Allah and the determined and spirited endeavors of the nation, the destiny of the country has fallen in the hands of the people and their true representatives are elected and sent to the parliament without foreign interference and intervention of government feudals, it is hoped that, all sorts of perversion would be stopped with their dedication to Islam and to the interests of the country. My recommendation to the present and future generation is to elect righteous, upright and educated candidates in every election. The candidates should be individuals committed to Islam and the Islamic Republic. Persons who come mostly from the deprived middle classes of the society and are neither perverted nor gone astray from the Straight Path; individuals who are aware of the problems of the nation and the laws and policies of Islam.

My advice to the honorable clerics, specially the religious authorities, is not to show indifference to parliamentary and presidential elections of the Islamic Republic. You all witnessed and future generations shall learn how politicians who were followers of the East and the West removed the clerics, who were greatly influential in laying the foundations of the Constitution in the country. They would come to realize how clerics were deceived by such politicians who inculcated in them that involvement in the affairs of the country and of the Muslims were outside the parameters of their holy position and status. Consequently, they relinquished the realm of politics to pro-West or pro-East elements who dealt with the Constitutional Law, the country, and Islam damages in a way that would take ages to remedy.

Now that the obstacles have been removed, no excuses would remain. A free atmosphere is made available to all to involve and participate in the affairs of the country. So it is an unforgivable sin to neglect the affairs of Muslims. Every individual should be available to serve Islam and the country to the extent possible. Everyone should try his best to prevent the influence of the pro-West and pro-East elements and those who deviate from the great school of Islam. All should realize that the opponents of Islam and Muslim countries or the superpowers and the international exploiters infiltrate into our country and into Islamic states cleverly and gradually and manipulate the people into colonialization. You must all be alert and vigilant. As soon as you discover such infiltration, you should not hesitate act to neutralize it. Give them no chance! May Allah help you!

I ask the present and the future representatives of the parliament to reject the credentials of any deviate delegate who has gained the votes of his constituents through fraud and political intrigues. Let no sabotaging element find his way into the parliament.

I advise the recognized religious minorities [1] to learn lessons from the situation of the parliament during the Pahlavi regime and elect representatives who are dedicated to their own religion and committed to the Islamic Republic of Iran, persons who are not dependent on the world-mongering powers, persons with no leaning towards any deviationist, forged or atheistic school of ideology.

I ask all parliament delegates to treat one another with utmost goodwill and brotherhood and be careful not to pass legislations contradictory to Islamic law. All of you should try to be faithful to Islam and its Divine law to earn prosperity in this world and in the Hereafter.

My advice to the Guardian Council,[2] now and in the future is to perform its Islamic and national duties with candor and take great care not to be influenced by any power and not to sanction any law, rule or regulation that is opposed to Islam and the Constitution. The Council should be attentive to the exigencies of the country that must be dealt with sometimes by secondary decrees and sometimes by the decrees of the Guardian of the Theologian or Jurisconsult.

My advice to the honorable nation is to participate actively in all parliamentary and presidential elections and those of the Assembly of Experts [3] to determine the Council of Leadership or the Leader.[1] The election

---

[1] Article 13 of the Constitutional Law of the Islamic Republic of Iran recognizes Zoroastrianism, Judaism and Christianity as true religious minorities who are free within the limits of law to perform their own religious rites and to act according to the dictates of their own faith in matters of personal status.

[2] In order to ensure the conformity of the legislation approved by the Majlis with tenets and teachings of the Holy Quran and the Constitution of the Islamic Republic of Iran, a council named Guardian Council being composed of 6 jurisprudents and 6 lay jurists or legal experts from various branches of the law was formed as provided by Article 92 of the Constitution. These men are elected for a period of 6 years (Article 92). The Islamic Consultative Assembly is not legally valid without the Guardian Council (Article 93). All legislation enacted and approved by the Majlis should be sent to the Guardian Council to confirm their conformity with Islamic laws (Article 94).

[3] In the system of the Islamic Republic of Iran, public affairs must be administered on the basis of public opinion and by means of elections. If in an election, whether presidential or parliamentary, etc. obtaining a majority of votes is not possible or if achieving a purpose

of such representatives should be based on solid and creditable criteria. For example, if election of the Assembly of Experts is not inconformity to religious laws and standards, irreparable damages would be inflicted on the religion and the country, in which case all would be responsible before Allah the Exalted.

Thus, non-participation in elections by the people ranging from religious jurists and authorities to bazaar people, workers, farmers, civil servants, etc. whether among the present or future generations indicates their irresponsibility towards the destiny of the country and Islam. In certain cases, any failure to participate in the affairs of the state and elections would be taken as capital sins. Therefore, all must bear in mind that "Prevention is better than cure." If necessary action is not taken in advance, control of affairs would get out of all hands. This is a reality we all have experienced after the Constitutional Regime was proclaimed in the country. No remedial action is more effective than the people, nationwide performing the task and duties assigned to them in accordance with the Islamic constitution and Islamic laws and standards. In parliamentary and presidential elections, voters should consult educated and open-minded persons. Such persons should be aware of the channels of action. They should not be affiliates of any superpower. They should be dedicated to Islam and the Islamic Republic and reputed for their virtues. Such consultation should also be entered into with dedicated and chaste clerics. Care should be taken to ensure that those elected as president of the Islamic state and as delegates to the parliament are individuals who have felt and experienced the conditions of the deprived and oppressed classes of the society and who are concerned about the well-being of such people. The president and the parliament deputies should not hail from high-ranking and land-mongering capitalist classes sunken in carnal pleasures and are unable to understand the bitterness and pains of the deprived, the barefoot and the oppressed people.

---

requires argumentation and discussion, in that case the people elect their trusted experts who convene in an assembly called the Assembly of Experts wherein they discuss the issues that are of concern to the people. Example: The Experts on the Constitutional Law, the Experts on the Leadership, etc.

[1] Whenever a qualified religious jurisprudent is recognized and confirmed by majority of the people as a Leader, such a leader and religious authority assumes all the responsibilities that ensue the title. If this does not materialize, the experts elected by the people study and consult among themselves the qualifications of all those who meet the standards set for leadership and from among them select three or five competent religious authorities and present them to the people as 'members of the Leadership Council'. In the review of the Constitutional Law of the Islamic Republic of Iran (IRI), this article was amended; the leadership council of the Muslim community is not envisaged.

We should realize that if the parliament delegates and the president are competent, devoted to Islam sympathetic with their fellow countrymen, most difficulties would not emerge. If they do, they will be solved without any delay. This also applies to the election of the Assembly of Experts to determine the Council of Leadership or the Leader. For, if the experts are elected by the nation with care and consultation with prominent religious jurists and authorities of the time, and if learned, dedicated, and virtuous persons go to the Assembly of Experts, because of the selection of the most competent individuals as the Council of Leadership or the Leader by them, then most of the major problems would not arise. In case it did, they would be dealt with efficiently. With regard to Articles 109 [1] and 110 [2] of the Constitution concerning the grave duty of the nation in electing the 'Experts' and the 'Delegates' to determine the Leader or the Council of Leadership, it becomes clear that the least oversight and negligence in their related elections would create gross harm to Islam, the country, and the Islamic Republic. Because of the paramount importance of the probability of their incidence, their occurrence surely entails Divine responsibility.

My advice to the Leader and the Council of Leadership in this era which is to dedicate themselves to the service of Islam and the deprived people of this country. They should not think that leadership is per se a gift or an exalted position for them. Rather, it should be thought of as a heavy and grave duty in which errors caused by mean and low considerations would subject the perpetrator to life-long shame in this world and to the wrath of Allah in the Hereafter.

I beg the Almighty God to admit us while we have to His emerged successful in this trial. This threat exists, though to a lesser degree, to presidents, governments and authorities now and in the future, each in

---

[1] Article 109 of the Constitution of the I.R.I. is devoted solely to a declaration of the qualities and qualifications of the leader and of the members of the Leadership Council. These terms or conditions include: academic competence, the necessary righteousness, political and social insight, courage and sagacity and sufficient administrative ability. These principles were modified somewhat in amendment to the Constitution under the heading of 'Conditions and Qualities of the Leader'.

[2] Article 110 of the Constitution of I.R.I. deals exclusively with the leader's powers and responsibilities, which mainly include: appointment of the *fuqaha* the members of the Guardian Council, appointment of the highest judicial authority of the country, appointment and removal of the commanders of the armed forces, introduction of the Supreme Defense Council, declaration of war and peace, endorsement of the credentials of the president following his election by people, removal of the president from office in a view of the country's interests, grant of amnesty to convicts or reduction of their sentences within Islamic rules. In amendment to the Constitution, this article has been somewhat modified.

proportion to their responsibility. They should also be mindful of the fact that God is present and oversees their actions. May Almighty God guide and protect them!

H. Justice is another essential issue to threat. It is involved with people's lives, properties and family chastities. My advice to the Leader and the Council of Leadership is to do their utmost in selection and appointment of highly qualified, deeply committed, dedicated persons and experts in Islamic law and politics for the relevant responsibilities.

I ask the Supreme Judicial Council [1] to clear up the woeful conditions in which all legal and judicial matters had sunk during the former regime, to cut off from this sublime tribune the hands of those who play games with the people's lives and properties, and those judges for whom Islamic justice has the least meaning. Try hard to change the Department of Justice gradually and appoint qualified judges whom the theology centers, especially the Qom Theological Seminary, train and introduce instead of judges who do not possess the required Islamic qualifications so that by Allah's will, Islamic justice would be implemented all over the country.

I advise the present and future judges to keep in mind the Islamic traditions ascribed to the Infallible Imams (s), regarding the importance of judging and great danger, which lurks behind the position of judging and unjust adjudication. They should not allow this position to go to people who do not deserve it. Those who are qualified for these positions should not reject to accept these appointments. Let those who qualify as magistrates assume the responsibility of this great task. Let all know that as the responsibility of adjudication is hazardous and great, its rewards and excellences are also considerable and grand. All should know that assuming the position of a judge is a religious duty.[2]

I. My advice to the holy theological seminaries, as I have often said, is that opponents of Islam and the Islamic Republic are determined to uproot Islam in every satanic way possible. A major approach they make towards their ominous objective which is dangerous to Islam and the theological seminaries, is to have deviate and corrupt individuals infiltrate into the

---

[1] This council, which was the highest judicial authority in the Judicial Power of the I.R.I., was deleted in the process of adding an amendment to the Constitution and the status of the country's highest judicial authority was vested in an individual person.
[2] An obligatory duty incumbent on every Muslim; if fulfilled by some members of the Islamic community it ceases to be obligatory to others.

seminaries. In the short run, this poses the danger of casting aspersion on the conduct of the students of theology, accusing them of having perverted and unethical behavior and character. Infiltration into theological seminaries by such evil agents poses a serious threat. Some of them may attain to high positions through their machinations. With the help of their sham knowledge of Islamic laws and rules, they may work their way into the confidence and hearts of the people and then at the right time deliver fatal blows to the seminaries, to Islam, and to the country. We are aware that the superpowers have implanted agents in various communities under different guises such as: 'nationalists', 'pan-Iranists', 'liberals', 'pseudo-intellectuals' and 'pseudo-clerics'. This last group, if given the opportunity, is highly insidious and dangerous. Such agents live, sometimes for decades, among nations with patience, Islamic pretentions, deportment, sham patriotism, and other designs and carry out their missions at the proper time during the short span of time. Since the triumph of the revolution, our people have seen such agents under the titles of *'Mujahid-e Khalq'*,[1] *'Fadai-ye Khalq'*,[2] *'Tudeh'*,[3] and other such

---

[1] The term *'Mujahid-e-Khalq'* literally means 'people's fighter' or 'one who struggles for the people'. However, in reality and in the political history of the Iranian nation, *'Mujahidin-e-Khalq'* is the name of a guerrilla or partisan fighter group that came to be in 1965 (1344 A.H.) to challenge the Shah. Due to the inadequacy of the familiarity of its leaders with the principles and all-inclusive teachings of the school of Islam, this organization adopted an eclectic ideology and, within a short time after the victory of the Islamic Revolution, took position opposite to the revolution. Its forces martyred a large number of people's true servants, the dedicated clerics and religious authorities and finest youths. They also detonated scores of bombs all over the country and burned houses and street buses full of passengers; they started a stream of running blood. This group spared nothing in fighting the Islamic Revolution but in the long run, after going through several stages, was suppressed by the revolutionary forces and some of them fled to foreign countries. Those who were once daubed anti-imperialism and afraid to have their identity revealed, are today spending their last shameful day in the laps of imperialists in utter ignominy. The terrorist group of *Mujahidin-e-Khalq* has been equated by the public with the 'hypocrites'.

[2] The *Fada'iyan-e Khalq* were a partisan or guerrilla Marxist group that started their political, terrorist, anti-revolutionary moves after the victory of the revolution. The group's birth dates back to 1966 when a number of Marxists student had gradually become disenchanted with Orthodox Marxism and leaned towards Maoism. In spite of their terrorist activities against the Shah's top brass, their popular base among the lay student and university leftists remained undeveloped; they were unable to gain public recognition. This group struggled for rapid institution of the socialist discipline in Iran. However, political and ideological crisis gradually divided this process into several branches. The Marxist's international crisis and the circumstances in the former Soviet Union deeply affected these elements and caused their political abashment.

[3] The *Tudeh* is the oldest Marxist-Leninist organization in Iran. Remnants of the communist party of Iran proclaimed existence in 1920. It began its activities in 1942 under the title of 'The *Tudeh* Party of Iran. Because of its direct affiliation in its political life with the former

appellations. It is necessary for the whole nation to cooperate in neutralizing such conspiracies. All should be alert to the danger of these agents. The purging of the theological centers takes priority. This is the task of the honorable scholars and teachers of Islamic texts and the well-known men of theological centers with the approval of the religious authorities of the time. Perhaps the thesis that "Order lies in disorderliness" is one of the vicious inspirations of these plotters.

At any rate, my advice is that at all times, especially at the present times it is necessary in which plots and intrigues have increased, it is necessary to rise and bring order to the seminaries. Let the canonists, the scholars, and the instructors spend time and, by careful, sound planning, purge and preserve the major theological centers, especially the Qum Theological Center.

It is necessary that the honorable and distinguished scholars and theologians prevent perversion and distortion from creeping into the teaching materials concerning religious jurisprudence. Let there be no deviation from the methods of the grand learned authorities of religious law in the teachings of the principles of jurisprudence. Only in this way can the real Islamic jurisprudence be preserved. Efforts should be made for a daily increase in the consciousness of views, investigative methods, research and creative work. Traditional jurisprudence, which is the heritage of our worthy ancestors, must be preserved and maintained, because deviation from it weakens the foundations of research. Let research studies in jurisprudence be increased and developed to the utmost. With respect to other sciences, to be sure, research programs should be arranged with a view to the needs of the country and Islam. Students should be trained to do research work at the highest levels and in as many areas as needed. Research, its learning, teaching, and practice must be made available to all. Islamic moral sciences such as ethics, ego-purging, mystical teachings, etc. should be covered in the course of such

---

Soviet intelligence Service, the *Tudeh* Party assumed positions that made it notorious as treacherous group. The most important of such positions was the *Tudeh* Party's support of the separation of Azarbayejan and Kordestan from Iran by the Soviet troops and its support of granting oil concession in the north of Iran to The Soviets. After the coup d'Âtat of August 19, 1953 and the continuation of Mohammad Reza Shah's monarchy, the activities of the *Tudeh* Party within Iran ceased until 1979 marking the victory of the Islamic Revolution in Iran. The central committee of the *Tudeh* Party was stationed in Leipzig, East Germany. With the victory of the Islamic Revolution, favorable grounds were provided for the party and other groups to resume activity. However, because of atheistic beliefs and hypocritical tactics, the *Tudeh* Party failed to find a firm base among the people in spite of years of struggle and propaganda. At last, in 1983, when espionage relations of this party with KGB and the former Soviet Military intelligence Services were reveled, the members of its central committee were apprehended and the party's secret networks were disbanded.

educational research. This is especially necessary with the 'Spiritual Journey', purification of the soul, and the ego known as 'Greater Crusade'. May Allah bestow it upon us!

J. One of the areas that need purging, reform and care is the Executive Power of the country. Sometimes beneficial and progressive laws are enacted by the parliament, seconded by the Guardian Council and communicated by the concerned cabinet minister to the proper administrative unit or department for implementation, but is thwarted by bureaucracy, by incompetent personnel, by open violation of rules and regulations. Such actions are sometimes deliberately taken to create dissatisfaction and anxiety in the community.

My advice to the related present and future cabinet ministers is that they and their employees are earning on public funds and should, therefore, be sincere public servants, especially to the deprived. Creating uneasiness for the public and not doing one's duties are interdicted and may incur the wrath of Allah. You all need the nation's support, especially that of the deprived classes. It was by their support that victory could be achieved and the hands of tyrants virtually cut off from the country and its wealth. If you become deprived from this support some day, the oppressors would put you aside and take your place just the way you ousted the oppressive monarchical regime. In view of these tangible facts, you should make efforts to satisfy the nation and earn their confidence. Avoid inhumane and un-Islamic conduct.

Following this motivation, I recommend that our state ministers in future take great care in selecting provincial governors. They should make certain that such men are competent, wise, agreeable and dedicated to Islam and the Islamic Republic and can get along with the people so that peace and tranquility would prevail throughout the country. It should be remembered that although every cabinet minister has the responsibility of Islamizing and regulating the affairs of his own area of responsibility, yet, some of them have special responsibility. Take, for example, the Ministry of Foreign Affairs, which is in charge of our embassies abroad. Since the early days after the victory of the revolution, I have often warned the ministers of foreign affairs about the pro-*Taghuti* nature of our embassies abroad and about the need for their purge and conversion into embassies worthy of the Islamic Republic. Some of them, however, either could not or did not want to take positive steps. Now that three years have passed since the victory of the revolution, the present Foreign Minister has undertaken this task and it is hoped that, by hard work and devotion this important matter can be accomplished in due time.

My advice to the present and future foreign ministers is that their responsibilities are heavy and sensitive indeed, whether in reforming your offices and embassies or in the area of foreign policy. You should preserve our independence and secure the interests of the country in the area of having suitable relations with the countries that do not intend to interfere in our internal affairs. Anything that might smack dependence in its various aspects and dimensions should be avoided. You should know that dependencies in some affairs, even though they may seem appealing and attractive in appearance, will result in the destruction of the roots of the country. Thus make every effort to improve relations with Islamic countries and to awaken their statesmen and invite all to unity and alliance. Know that Allah is with you.

My advice to Muslim nations is: Do not look for outside help in achieving your goal, which is Islam and implementation of the Islamic rules. You yourselves should rise up and undertake this vital issue, which will make liberty and independence a reality. Let the grand religious authorities and honorable preachers in Islamic states call on their governments to extricate themselves from dependence on superpowers and come to an understanding with their own nations, in which they would embrace victory. They should invite nations to unity and alliance and avoid racism, which is contrary to the teachings of the Holy Quran. They should shake hands in friendship with their fellow believers in any country and race, since the great Islamic faith has termed them all 'brothers'. If, by Allah's Grace, this spirit of brotherhood-in-faith is realized, you will see that one day the Muslims constitute the world's greatest power. God willing, this brotherhood and equality may manifest itself soon.

My advice to the Ministry of Culture and Islamic Guidance at all times, especially at the present with its own particular characteristics, is to propagate the truth versus falsehood and to present the reality of the Islamic Republic. Now that we have virtually cut off the hands of the superpowers from our country we are subjected to enormous propaganda aggression of all mass media organizations dependent on the superpowers. Consider the baseless accusations leveled against us by the writers and speakers of these mass media apparatus subservient to the superpowers.

Regrettably, most of the Islamic states of the region that should show us brotherhood, by the command of Islam have risen in opposition to us and to Islam. They have placed themselves at the service of the superpowers for invasion against us from every side and quarter. It is to be mentioned that our propaganda mechanism is very weak while the world today revolves around publicity and propaganda. The so-called intellectual writers are either pro-West or pro-East. Their selfishness and monopolism do not let them think of independence and freedom of their own country. These factors do not allow the writers to consider the interests of their own nation and draw comparison between freedom and independence in the Islamic Republic today with that in the former tyrannical regime. Such writers and speakers do not stop to weigh and measure the worthy and honorable life in this country today against the partial losses in comfort and physical pleasures. In time of the former regime they were indulged in pleasure seeking, dependency, servitude, praising, and eulogizing those nuclei of corruption and vice. Foregoing this, they would desist from bringing such false and totally inaccurate accusations against this newly-born Islamic Republic. They would use their pens and tongues against the *taghut*s in favor of this nation and government.

The issue of propaganda is not only the function of the Ministry of Culture and Islamic Guidance. Rather, it is a duty incumbent on all writers, speakers, artists and scholars. The Ministry of Foreign Affairs should see to it that the embassies are supplied with public relations literature to reveal the briliant image of Islam to all the world. If the glorious and immaculate image of Islam, which the Holy Quran and the Tradition have invited all to their various dimensions, would emerge from under the veils by the opponents of Islam ignorant friends, Islam would overwhelm the whole world and its banner of honor unfurled everywhere. How tragic it is that, the Muslims possess the most valuable gem, unparalleled in the world from its very commencement to the end of the world, yet being not only have unable to present this Divine gift, which every human being aspires by nature. They themselves are negligent and ignorant of its value and sometimes run away from it.

K. One of the most important and fateful issues is the question of educational institutions from kindergarten to university. Because of its far-reaching importance, I repeat the matter in passing. The pillaged nation should know that during the past fifty years, all the devastating blows to Iran and Islam have been mainly dealt with universities. If universities and other centers of learning and education were engaged in educating, purifying and training the youth armed with Islamic and patriotic programs for the benefit of the country, our country would have never been swallowed first by

England and then by America and Russia. Such ruinous agreements or treaties would not have been imposed on our deprived nation. Nor would foreign advisers have been admitted to the country. Our resources, including the black gold would never go down the pockets of the satanic powers. Similarly, the Pahlavi family and its dependents could not have plundered the people's wealth and build for themselves at home and abroad private parks and villas over the bodies of the oppressed people. Foreign banks could not become rich with the wages of our deprived people and such funds would not have been spent by the *Taghut* and his offsprings and kinsmen on carnal whims and debauchery. If the parliament, the government, the judiciary power and other organs had come from Islamic national universities, our nation would have not been facing these ruinous problems today. If chaste personalities, with sound Islamic and nationalistic inclinations, not like that which is offered as Islam today, were dispatched from the universities to the three centers of power: 1(the legislative power, 2(the judiciary power, and 3(the executive power, we would be in different circumstances. We could see different days and our homeland would not be like this. Our deprived people would have been liberated; the cruelty and oppression of the monarchy would have been foiled by people much sooner as would the centers of vice, addiction and pleasure houses, one of which was enough to corrupt a whole generation of our young people. This disastrous legacy would not have been left for our people. If our universities were Islamic, humane and nationalistic, they would have trained, educated and presented to the society hundreds and thousands of teachers and professors. How sad it was that these institutions were administered and our children trained and educated, with a few exceptions, by people who were either Westernized or Easternized. These persons were installed in vital positions with special planning and design. Our dear, oppressed and innocent children were unfortunately trained by such wolves affiliated with the superpowers. They occupied high legislative, executive and judiciary positions and carried out the orders of the tyrannical Pahlavi regime.

Now that by the will of Allah, the Exalted, universities have been liberated from the grip of criminals, it behooves the nation and Islamic governments at all times not to permit corrupt elements, who are either the followers of deviant schools of thought or lean toward the West or the East, to influence the colleges, universities or the centers of education. Make guards against such individuals from the beginning and before they have achieved any mischievous plan.

My advice to the students of the teachers training centers, colleges and universities is to rise bravely and oppose all deviation and perversion so that their and the nation's independence and freedom would remain safe and secure.

L. The entire armed forces, including the army, navy, air force, *Sepah*, police, *Basij* volunteers the enlisted tribal militia enjoy special status. They are the mighty arms of the Islamic Republic. There are also the border guards. These forces ensure the safety of the roads, towns and rural areas. Indeed, they provide peace and security for the nation; therefore, they are entitled to receive special attention by the nation, the government, and the parliament. All should remember that the armed forces are manipulated and taken advantage of more than any other group or institutions by the superpowers with their destructive policies. It is through the armed forces that the superpowers carry out their political intrigues and arrange coups d'etat thus changing governments and regimes. The treacherous profiteers buy off some heads and commanders of such forces and, through them, work out their vicious conspiracies. They take over a country or dominate some oppressed nation, stripping them of their freedom and independence. If military commanders are upright and chaste, there can be no occasion for a military coup d'etat in a country, nor for its occupation. If any such moves are taken, they occur, will be defeated or neutralized by the dedicated commanders. In Iran, where the Islamic Revolution this miracle of the age, was performed by the nation, the devoted and committed armed forces and their pious and patriotic commanders had a considerable part in it.

But, today, the accursed war imposed by Saddam Takriti at the instigation, order, and through the assistance of the U.S.A. and other powers have met with the political and military defeat of the aggressive Bathist army after two years, its strong supporters and allies. The armed forces, security police, public militia and *Sepah* with unsparing help of the people have brought us honor at both the battlegrounds and behind the front lines. The internal intrigues and acts of mutiny by the puppets of the West or the East aimed at overthrowing the Islamic Republic were defeated by the youth of the Revolutionary Committees, Revolutionary Guards, mobilized volunteers, and police with the help of the nation. It is these zealous youths who stay awake at nights so that families may rest in peace. May Allah help and assist them!

Therefore, in these last few steps left to the end of my life, my brotherly advice to the armed forces who love Islam, who give their lives at the war fronts for the love of gaining proximity to God, and who carry out their devotional work everywhere in the country, is that you stay alert and vigilant and beware the treacherous political ruses of the pro-West or pro-East elements at play behind the scenes! Rest assured that the sharp edges of their blades are, from every side, directed at you more than at any other time. They want to make use of you, who have given your lives so that the revolution could triumph and Islam revived. They intend to overthrow the Islamic Republic. By shamming Islam and pretending to serve the country and the nation, they mean to separate you from Islam and the nation. They work to toss you down into the laps of one of the two world-mongering poles, they attempt to foil your efforts and sacrifices by political tricks.

My emphatic counsel to the armed forces is to observe and abide by the military rule of noninvolvement in politics. Do not join any political party, group or fraction. No military man or security policeman, no revolutionary Guard or *Basiji* is allowed to enter politics. Stay away from politics. You will be able to preserve and maintain your military powers and thus immune from internal division and dispute. Military commanders should prevent the men under their commands from entering into political parties. As the revolution belongs to all the nation, its preservation is also the duty of all. Therefore, the government, the nation, the Defense Council and the Islamic Consultative Assembly are all charged with the religious and national responsibility to oppose from the very beginning any interference in politics or any action against the interests of Islam and the country by the armed forces, regardless of category, class, branch, and rank. Such involvement will surely corrupt and pervert them. It is incumbent on the Leader and the Leadership Council to prevent such involvement of the armed forces by decisive action so that no harm would befall the country.

My sincere advice to all the armed forces in these last days of my earthly life is to remain faithful to Islam, as you are faithful to it now. Islam is the only true ideology of liberty and independence and Almighty God invites us all to attain to the exalted status of humanity by the light of Islam. Islam saves you, the country, and the nation from the shame of dependency and leaning on powers that desire slavery for you only. It desire to keep your country and your cherished nation retarded and as a consumer market under the yoke of subjugation. You should prefer an honorable life with difficulties to comfort and pleasure gained through slavery for strangers. You should know that as long as you extend your hands begging for advanced industrial needs, the power of initiative and inventiveness will not bloom in you. An objective example you witnessed after the economic blockade was those that seemed to be unable to make or repair anything. They were impelled to use their minds and brains and succeeded in manufacturing a good many things that met the needs of the army and the manufacturing plants. This war, the economic blockade and the expulsion of foreign specialists were divine blessings in disguise of which we were negligent. Now, if the government and the army would boycott the products of the world-mongers and make more effort to encourage inventiveness, the country may become self-sufficient and does not have to beg anything from the enemy.

After such prolonged artificial backwardness, our need for foreign-manufactured goods is an undeniable fact. This, however, does not mean that we should become dependent either of the two poles in advanced sciences. The government and army should send the students who are committed to Islam to countries that command advanced technology but are not colonizers or exploiters. They should not send students to America or Russia or to countries that follow these two poles. Perhaps, by the will of Allah, the day shall come when these powers see their mistakes and fall in the line of philanthropy, humanism and respect for the rights of others. Or, by the will of Allah, the oppressed people, alert nations and devout Muslims make them see their positions. May that day come!

M. Radio, television, the print media, cinema, and theaters are the most effective means for stupefying and corruption of nations, especially the younger generations. During the past century, especially the second half of it, great plots were hatched and executed through these media against Islam and its faithful servants, the clerics. The mass media are used also in the colonial propaganda networks of the West and the East. They have been used to create markets for goods, especially for the sale of luxury and decorative commodities. The media are focused on making people imitate other cultures, particularly in areas like clothing, consumption of alcoholic drinks, styles of architecture and in many other things. To look Westernized was the thing of which one should be proud. Especially, ladies in higher or middle income groups imitated the westerners in all forms and manners, in attire, in talking, in deportment, in all facets of behavior and in social relations. Foreign words and terms were used in speeches and writings in such a way as to be difficult to comprehend by most people, even by the peers of their users. Television films depicting Western or Eastern products made young men and women stray from the normal course of their work, sliging life and industry into oblivion irrespective of themselves and their personalities. They produced pessimism in people vis-à-vis their own beings, their country, culture and even about highly valuable works of art and literature of the West and the East through the treachery of middlemen and collectors. Magazines printed pictures and articles detrimental to morality. Newspapers took pride in directing the youth towards the West or the East by publishing anti-Islamic and anti-indigenous culture and articles. Extensive publicity promoted centers of vice like pleasure houses, gambling, casinos and lotteries. Large retail stores sold luxury goods, cosmetics, alcoholic beverages, etc. All this came to the country financed by export of oil, gas and other valuable minerals. If the Pahlavi regime had survived, our youths would have been ruined before long. These children of Islam and the country, who are the nation's hope for the future, would have been lost by the satanic conspiracies of that corrupt regime and through the mass media and pro-West or pro-East liberals and intellectuals. Or, they would have ruined their own lives in the centers of vice or turned stooges of the superpowers and destroyed the country. Almighty God has, by His Mercy, saved us from the mischief of evil-doers.

My advice to the Islamic Consultative Assembly, to Presidents, to the Guardian Council, to the Supreme Judicial Council and to Governments, now and in the future, is to maintain the news agencies, the press and the magazines in the service of Islam and the interests of the country. We must all know that Western-style freedom degenerates the youth and is therefore condemned in Islam's view and by intellect. Propaganda literature, articles, speeches, books and magazines that oppose Islam, public morality and the interests of the country are forbidden and their suppression is incumbent on us and on all other Muslims. Harmful liberties must be restrained. If all that is 'forbidden' and against the path of the nation, the Islamic state, the country and the prestige of the Islamic Republic is not decisively controlled, then all are to be held responsible. If people and the Hezbollah youth (lit., the members of the Party of Allah) encounter with a violation of these rules, they should report it to the appropriate authorities. If they fail to act, then the people themselves should take preventive measure. May Allah, the Exalted, help all!

N. My advice to the bands, groups, and persons especially their ringleaders abroad or at home, actively opposing the nation, the Islamic Republic and Islam, is that long experience whether acting in conspiracy in different ways or in asking foreign authorities and states for support, should have taught you. You regard yourselves wise and know that the direction of a self-sacrificing and dedicated nation cannot be altered by acts of terror, sabotage, explosion of bombs, spread of meaningless lies and baseless rumors. No state or government can ever be toppled by such inhumane and illogical methods, particularly a nation like that of Iran, whose youth, old men, women and children all sacrifice their lives in the path of the Holy Quran, their religion as well as the Islamic Republic. You should know - and you will be thinking naively if you do not - that the nation is not with you and that the army is against you. If you assume that they are with you, your crude moves and the acts of crime perpetrated by you, have caused separation between you and them. You have gained nothing but the enmity of others.

As a well-wisher, my advice to you at the close of my days is that: you are fighting an oppressed nation that after 2500 years of suffering, under the tyrannical rule, liberated itself by sacrificing the lives of its finest children and youth from the yoke of the oppressive Pahlavi regime and the world-mongering East and West. How can the conscience of a man allow him to behave so cruelly and mercilessly with his nation and country only for the sake of probability of gaining political power?! I advise you to give up such useless and unwise actions and not be fooled by the world-mongers. If you have not committed any crime, you can come back from wherever you are and submit yourselves to the fostering lap of Islam. You should repent to Allah, the Most Compassionate and the Most Forgiving and by the Will of Allah, the nation and the Islamic Republic may pardon you. If you have committed a crime for which Divine punishment is decreed, you should return to Him from the middle of the way and repent. If you courage, you should accept your punishment and thereby save your soul from the painful chastisement ordained by Allah. You should not waste your lives any longer; you should change your attitude; you should do something that is best for you.

Then, I ask the followers of these groups, whether domestic or foreign, why you ruin your lives and the life of the youth. These people who, as has been proven, are at the service of world powers, follow their plots and unknowingly have fallen in their traps? Why do you do wrong about your own nation? What for and for whom? They have been manipulated and fooled by the world powers. If you live here in this country, you can see with your own eyes that these multi-million strong masses are faithful to the Islamic Republic and are dedicated to it. You can see that the present government is most sincerely serving the people and the oppressed people. Those groups and bands who falsely claim that they belong to the people or are *Mujahid* or *Fadai*s have actually risen in opposition to Allah's servants.

Young boys and girls have been deceived by these groups, to serve their own objectives or the objectives of one of the two world-mongering poles, while themselves live in pleasure in the lap of one of these two poles of crime. Or, they live in luxury and comfort of elegant team-houses or residential villas and continue their crimes for which they sacrifice their lives.

My kind advice to you, the youth, who live in this country or abroad, is to give up the wrong path. Return and join up with the deprived people of the country who are serving the Islamic Republic wholeheartedly. Act to serve the free and independent Iran, so that the country and the nation may be rid of the enemy's sedition and mischief. Live in honor altogether and unitedly. Why and how long do you want to listen to the commands of leaders of the bands and groups who fight their own nation with the support of superpowers that think of nothing except their own personal gain, immolating you for their sinister aims? You have noted since the victory of the revolution, that their words and deeds are two different things. Their claims are made to deceive pure-hearted youths. You know you have no power vis-à-vis the torrential movement of the nation. Your actions can result only in the loss of your own lives. Hereby I have discharged my duty to advice you through my last will and testament. I hope you will listen to it and act upon it when it reaches you after my death. Then, there can be no question of personal gain and power-seeking motives on my part. By listening to these advices deliver yourselves from the painful chastisement decreed by God. May God, the Merciful, guide you to the straight path!

My advice to the groups such as communists, guerillas and other leftists is that without prior study about various schools of thought and consulting the authorities on Islam, how could you bring yourselves to embrace an ideology that is already dead? What was your incentive? What did make your hearts settle for "isms" that have already been proved null and void by researchers? What is your purpose in pushing your country to the lap of the Soviet Union or China? What do make you fight against your own nation in the name of 'love for the masses or make plots against your own people for the benefit of foreigners?' You see very well that those, who claimed and adhered to Communism since its inception, have been and still are the most dictatorial, power-hungry, hegemonist authorities and governments. How many a nation has not been crushed under the Soviet Union's pressure. Yet, the Soviets claim they are supporters of the masses. The people of the Soviet Union, Muslims or non-Muslims, are all struggling and writhing under the pressure of the Communist Party and suffering under a suffocating censorship that is worse than the censorship exercised by any other dictatorial governments. We witnessed coming to power of Stalin[1] and his stepping down and luxurious and aristocratic manner. He was one of the most distinguished faces of the party. Even now that you, the deceived individuals of this country, are ready to sacrifice your lives out of your love for the Communist Party of the Soviet Union, their deprived people and its satellites such as the people of Afghanistan, etc. are perishing under the Soviet regime's cruelty. Meanwhile, you, who claim to be siding with the masses, hurt and harm your own people in any possible way. You committed unimaginable crimes against the respectable people of Amol whom you had erroneously regarded as your staunch supporters and, by deception, sent many of them to fight the Muslim people and the Islamic government as a result of which many of your comrades were killed. [2] You, who claim to be supporters of the people, want to hand over the innocent and deprived people of Iran to the Soviet dictatorship. For this, you disguise yourselves as *Fadaiyan-e-Khalq* and supporters of the oppressed. Now, this is being carried out by the *Tudeh* Party and its cohorts by weaving plottings and intrigues under the guise of supporting the Islamic Republic and by other leftists groups using arms, terrors, bombings, etc.

---

[1] Joseph Stalin was a member of the Central Committee of the Bolshevik Party and a director of the Pravda Newspaper, the official organ of the former Soviet Communist Party. In 1922, Stalin was elected as Secretary General of the party. He was then actually placed at the head of the Soviet government. The story of Stalin's cow has often been referred to by Imam Khomeini in his talks. The story is about the Tehran Conference of the heads of the allies during World War II. It is related that the Anglo-American heads of state, in spite of their imperialistic beliefs, had not much observed formalities and protocols while Joseph, in spite of his proletarian background, had brought a cow to Tehran with him in his aircraft so as to have his own exclusive fresh milk every morning. Such attachments and such proletarian slogans that are in sharp contrast and mutually contradictory are the sort of things Imam Khomeini has often recalled.

[2] An incident was perpetrated in Amol, a city in the north of Iran, by a group called 'Communist Union'. This group, which was a small Maoist group, had no activity inside Iran during the time of the Shah. However, as soon as the revolution triumphed, elements of the group entered the country from the U.S.A. and Western Europe and started their activity in Amol. During this incursion, nearly 50 armed elements of this group who were committing terrorist acts against Iran in the forests of the north, entered the city of Amol in a calculated and planned act. The objective of these terrorists was the military occupation of the city. They had figured that if they took the city, the people of surrounding territory would join them and thus an insurgent base against Islamic Revolution would be set up. Contrary to their fancy, the people of the city spontaneously resisted this armed invasion from its onset and the city became the battleground of intense fighting between the unarmed defenders and the armed men of the group. After 5 hours of fighting, all the invading elements were captured or slained by the people and the plot was defused. A considerable number of defenseless men, women and children were also killed in this incident.

I advise the political parties and groups, whether those known as leftists-although indications point to their affiliation with American communists—or those who receive their sustenance as well as their inspiration from the West, to join their own nation. This also holds true of those who, are taking up arms and ruin the lives of the deprived people of Kurdistan[1] and other localities in the name of 'self-rule' and support for the Kurds[2] and Baluchis,[3] you have thus thwarted the Islamic government's efforts to implement educational, medical and economic services as well as reconstruction activities in those provinces. I similarly advise the Komoleh[4] and Democrat [5] Parties, whose activities thus far show that they have done nothing but harm and bringing nothing but misery to those areas. Therefore, it is to their own benefit as well as to the benefit of their nation and their provinces to cooperate with the government, avoid insurgency and refrain from serving the foreigners and doing treason to the country. Rather, they should participate in the country's reconstruction and rest assured that Islam is better for them than the criminal West or the dictatorial East. Islam can better fulfill man's wishes.

My advice to the Muslim groups, who have mistakenly acquired 'Westward' or 'Eastward' leanings and sometimes supported the *Munafiqin*

---

[1] A province inhabited by Iranian Kurds, located in the west of the country.
[2] One of the Iranian ethnic people who mostly live in western provinces.
[3] One of the Iranian ethnic people living in eastern provinces, mostly in Sistan and Baluchistan.
[4] Immediately after the victory of the Islamic Revolution in Iran, the Komoleh Group, consisting of a number of adventurous anarchists with an ideology leaning toward Maoism, was founded. According to existing documents, this group was instantly placed under serious material and military protection and support of Western intelligence services, especially those of England and its dependent Baghdad regime. The reputation of the Komoleh was mostly due to its brutal torture savage killings of the people and defendants of the revolution.
[5] Another ethnic-minded group that undertook armed and terrorist actions against the revolution, after it had triumphed, was the Democrats of Kordestan of Iran. The Democratic Party was formed in 1945 when a part of the Iranian territory was under the occupation of the Soviet troops. It framed an autonomous government in Kordestan on the strength of the Soviet army. After the withdrawal of the Soviet troops from Iran, this party had no actual existence but its name or title was retained by the pro-Soviet Party, the *Tudeh*. In the meantime a member of the *Tudeh* Party named Qasimlu was able to obtain a Ph.D. degree through one of the scholarships that the Checkoslovak government made available to the *Tudeh* Party. Qasimlu meanwhile married a Jewish Check lady.
On the basis of available document Qasimlu was engaged in intelligence relations through his wife with the Israel intelligence services. After a while, he migrated to Baghdad and continued the publication of the new series of the magazine termed 'Kordestan', with the help of the Bath Party of Iraq. With the victory of the Islamic Revolution in Iran, Qasimlu quickly entered the Kordestan of Iran announced the start of the Islamic Revolution in Iran, and 'ethnic autonomy' in the Revolutionary Iran.

(hypocrites), whose treason was proven, is not persist in making such mistakes. Let these groups and individuals show Islamic courage and admit their mistakes. Please Allah, line up behind the government and the parliament join the people. All together rescue the oppressed people from the mischief and wickedness of the oppressors. Remember what that great Muslim jurist, Mudarris [1] said at a sad parliament meeting of his time: "Now that we must be destroyed, why do we do it ourselves?"

In memory of that great martyr of Allah, I say to you today that it is much better we be eradicated from the surface of the earth with honor by the treacherous hands of America and Russia and meet our Allah in glory than to live in comfort and luxury under the flag of the Red Army of the East or under the flag of the Black Army of the West. Such has been the practice of Allah's great Prophets, Infallible Imams and the men of religion. This is also the line we should follow. We should bring ourselves to believe that if a nation wants to, it can survive without any dependency and that world powers cannot impose anything against a nation's resolution.

A lesson should be learned from Afghanistan. While that usurping government and the leftist parties had and still have the Soviet Union on their side, they have not been able to suppress the people. Moreover, today, the deprived nations of the world have awakened and soon enough their

---

[1] Mudarris is regarded, in the history of Iran, a champion of freedom, a pro-independence cleric and a fighter against dictatorship. He was born in 1886, in a village and received his elementary education in Isfahan and his higher education in the holy city of Najaf. Simplicity and easy to understand parlance, kindness of temper and disposition as well as simple living, placed Mudarris in a position of leadership and guidance among the people. During the second legislative session of the National Consultative Assembly of Iran in 1949, Mudarris was elected by the religious scholars and clerics of Najaf and Iran as one of the five religious jurisprudents to supervise the enactment of laws. At the end of the 2nd session of the Majlis, Mudarris was elected as a delegate representing Tehran. Mudarris was opposed to puppet governments and their treacherous anti-nationalistic action and the agreement signed with England in 1919, the ratification of which he presented in the Majlis. Because of all this, Mudarris and his supporters were arrested by the command of the British through Reza Khan, commander of the Cossack Brigade. They were imprisoned and tortured. Public pressure and demonstration led to their release after 3 months of imprisonment service. In the Majlis, Mudarris disclosed Reza Khan's plan for republic form of government for Iran. This and his opposition to the rule of Reza Khan who acted according dictats of the British government helped Mudarris to be recognize as the most steadfast figure of anti-colonialism and anti-dictatorship.
Foreigners and their puppets who were mortified by the influence of Mudarris and saw that the plots to terrorize him fell through one after the other, decided to smother this vociferous and clear call to Islam and liberty. Therefore, they prepared plans to apprehend and deport him and finally, one day in the month of Ramadan 1316 [1937], they poisoned this great scholar while in a state of fasting and then strangulated him.

consciousness shall result in uprisings, movements, insurgencies and revolutions. They shall liberate themselves from the domination of the arrogant oppressors. You, Muslims, who care for Islamic values can well see that keeping away from the West or the East is revealing its blessings. Native intellects and minds have become active and are moving in the direction of self-sufficiency. All that the treacherous specialists of the West or the East claimed to be impossible for Iranian people to achieve is markedly achieved by the hands and brains of the nation. By Allah's will the trend shall continue in the future. Alas, this revolution took place rather late! Had it taken place even as early as the beginning of Muhammad Reza's rule, this pillaged country would have been something else today.

My advice to the writers, orators, intellectuals, fault-finders and those with inferiority complex is to reflect one night on what you are doing. You are spending your time pursuing a course contrary to that of the Islamic Republic and doing all you can to vitiate the parliament, the government and other public servants with your pessimism and ill-will, thereby pushing your country into the path of superpowers. Sit one night in seclusion with your Allah; if you do not believe in Allah, sit in seclusion with your conscience, and study your inner motives, of which people are often unaware. Think of the reason why and by what standard of fairness you ignore the blood of all young martyrs strewn everywhere on the battlefields and in towns and cities throughout the country. Why have you started a psychological war against a nation that has shaken off its neck the pressures of foreign and domestic oppressors and plunderers and has paid dearly for its freedom and independence with the blood of its beloved youth and now wants to preserve it with further sacrifice? Why do you reopen the way for the arrogant oppressors by brewing treacherous plots and by creating discord and disunity? Is it not better that you guide the government, the parliament and the nation by your pens, words and minds in order to preserve your homeland? Are the deprived not worth of your assistance? Is it not better that you try to support the Islamic government? Do you regard this parliament, this president, this government and this judicial system worse than what we had in the former regime? Have you forgotten the cruelty with which the former regime treated this oppressed nation? Are you not aware that this Islamic country was a military base for the US and was, in effect, a US colony? Do you not know that the parliament, the government and the military forces were under the US control? Do you not know that foreign specialists, advisors, and industrialists played havoc with this nation and its resources? Have you forgotten the spread of immorality throughout the country nationwide, centers of vice including gambling, bars, nightclubs, liquor stores, cinemas, etc.? Each one of these was a major cause of corruption of the youth! Have you forgotten the pornography which was encouraged by the corrupt mass media during the former regime? Now that the vice markets do not exist, are you crying in protest for trial of several young men. They were mostly from deviant and pervert groups, who had acted to defile and tarnish Islam and the Islamic government by their terroristic acts. Are you protesting the execution of a number of people who had revolted against Islam and the Islamic Republic? You befriend individuals who have overtly condemned Islam and have risen against it with the 'sword' or with their pens and tongues which are more dangerous than armed struggle. You have made friends with people such as these and shake hands with them as brothers! You call individuals whose blood is lawful to be shed, the apple of your eyes! You sit beside these 'actors' and watched them create the carnage of 14th of Isfand[1] (March 5, 1981) calamity in which the youth were beaten up. You then call such acts Islamic and ethical! But, when the government and the courts of justice rightly punish the enemies and the atheistic perverts, you cry out in protest and claim that these perverts are innocent! I feel sorry for you brothers with whose past I am somewhat familiar, and like some of you. I do not feel sorry for those who were evil-doers draped in the clothes of benevolence, those wolves in the clothes of sheep. These game players fool around, making fun of everyone. They were intent on destroying the country and the nation. All the time they were in the service of either of the two plundering poles. Those, who martyred our valuable young men, our cherished religious authorities, educators and instructors of the community with their filthy hands in fact deprived themselves from Allah's Mercy. They showed no mercy toward innocent Muslim children and thus have no way of return, as they are governed by their devilish self.

But why you, the believers, do not aid the government and the parliament that are trying to serve the oppressed and the barefooted people who are deprived of all facilities? What is your complaint? What does ail you? Have you thought of evaluating the amount of service rendered by this government and by the various foundations of the republic in comparison with limited development of the previous regime? All these were accomplished despite the imposed war with all its damages, destruction, millions of local and foreign refugees, with all acts of sabotage in a relatively short time. Do you

---

[1] It refers to a violence between leftist groups and Hezbollah which resulted in martyrdom of several innocent young men.

not know that the development programs and works in the former regime were confined, almost entirely, to cities and that to well-off areas and people? The poorer classes had little or no share of it, whereas the present regime and the Islamic foundations wholeheartedly serve the deprived groups. You believers, support the government so that projects are accomplished faster. Thus, when you eventually appear in God's presence you are marked with the sign of service to His servants.

O. One of the issues that requires comment is that Islam does not support oppressive and uncontrolled capitalism which deprives the masses. The Book and the Tradition seriously condemn this type of capitalism and regard it as opposed to social justice. Although some have wrongly thought that Islam favors uncontrolled form of capitalism, that is not true! Such malreasoning veils the shining face of Islam and paves the way for biased attacks of the enemies of Islam. They consider it as a capitalist regime on the order of the U.S.A., England and other Western plunderers. Relying on such baseless accusations and wrong understanding, the enemies rise to challenge Islam without referring to Islamic sources for clarification of the point. Islam does not oppose private the ownership, like Communism, Marxism, and Leninism. From the earliest days until now these schools have taken a variety of forms. They sanction homosexuality and sharing of spouses. They have always been accompanied by dictatorship.

Rather, Islam is a balanced and moderate school that recognizes ownership and respects it in a limited form of production and consumption. If it is implemented, a sound economy and social justice would result from it, for social equity is a prerequisite to having a healthy regime. Here, too, a number of unaware and illogical persons with no knowledge of Islam and its ideas for a healthy economy, have risen in opposition to the first group. By appealing to some Quranic verses and reciting phrases from the *Nahj al-Balaghah*, they consider Islam as being in agreement with the deviationist schools such as Marxism and his peers. Such men do not pay attention to the other parts of the *Nahj al-Balaghah* and the Quranic verses. As a result of their inadequate understanding, they have risen to follow a communist idea. They ignore the inherent atheism, dictatorship and strangulation of human values by a minority party treating human masses as animals!

I advise the parliament, the Guardian Council, the Government, the president and the Supreme Judicial Council to be obedient to the commands of Allah and not to be influenced by the inane propaganda of the cruel, rapacious pole of capitalism and the atheistic pole of communism and to respect ownership and private capital within Islamic limits. I advise you to reassure the nation so that private and creative initiatives proliferate in order to make the country and government reach self-sufficiency in all areas including light and heavy industries.

I advise those who lawfully acquire wealth to invest their legitimately gained wealth for innovative development works in agriculture, rural development and industries. This in itself is a commendable act of worship.

I advise all people to make ceaseless efforts for the welfare of the deprived classes. This is considered as good deeds both in this world and the Hereafter. These groups have suffered throughout the long and oppressive feudal and monarchical history. How fair it would be if the wealthy classes could voluntarily provide housing and other relief aids to the slum-dwellers. It will be a blessing to them on earth and in the Hereafter. It is far from fairness that one person owns scores of buildings while scores of other people of his community is deprived of a single room where in to live.

P. I have a piece of advice to the pseudo-clerics who oppose the Islamic Republic and devote their time to uproot it. They help the enemy carry out its plots and political intrigues. As has been reported, they make large financial contributions provided by Godless capitalists to sabotage works. You have gained nothing so far from your wrong-doings. I think, you will not achieve anything. Thus, if you do all these evil acts for the sake of gaining in this world, God shall not let you gain anything. It is better for you, then, to repent while there is a chance. Beg for God's forgiveness and join ranks with the oppressed nation. Support the Islamic Republic, which has found reality by the sacrifices of the nation. However, I do not think you will repent.

To those clerics who are against the Islamic Republic and who make every effort to overthrow it I say you had better make a comparison between the two regimes in your private. You think this regime is worse than the monarchy or similar to it. Your judgments are mostly based on the complaints received from wrong-doers opposed to Islam. Think about the Islamic Republic with sincerity in your seclusion. Make a fair and impartial comparison between it and the former regimes and consider that world revolutions have all entailed disruption, riots, confusion and disturbances. Opportunists always struggle to take advantage of such conditions for their own selfish aims. Consider the fact that the Islamic Republic faced all these. It had to withstand false accusations, propaganda, lies and armed attacks from outside and inside of its borders. It had to fight the unavoidable infiltration of corrupt and anti-Islamic elements, who were trying government organs, to generate dissatisfaction and unrest. Moreover, most of the public servants in the regime were inexperienced; many old-timers were dissatisfied because of their resentment by spreading lies and baseless rumors. All this, plus a shortage of judges, strenuous economic entanglements, difficulties in purging corrupt personnel and a shortage of qualified and competent personnel and many other problems had to be and were dealt with. On the other hand, biased monarchists, with immeasurable capital acquired by usury, foreign exchange manipulations, profiteering, exorbitant commodity prices, extortionist rates of services, smuggling, hoarding, and similar evil acts place the deprived classes under extreme pressure and draw the society to vice and disintegration. Men of this category come to you with deceptive purposes. To make you believe what they say, they sham Islam and even pay the Imam's share and shed false tears. They enrage and incite you to opposition. Many of these individuals sponge the people's blood or exploit them by some illegitimate ways and means and make the country's economy go bankrupt.

My brotherly, humble advice is that you, honorable people, be not influenced by rumors. Support and strengthen this republic for the sake of Allah and for the preservation of Islam. Be sure that if the Islamic regime falls, a republic acceptable to Imam of the Time and pleasant to you would not be realized. Rather, a regime acceptable to either one of the two power poles would replace it much to the disappointment of the world's deprived peoples who have turned to Islam and the Islamic government. Islam shall become isolated for ever and you would regret your conduct some day when it is too late! If you, gentlemen, expect all things to be Islamized overnight, you are making a mistake. Such miracle has never happened in any part of history of mankind. When the Great Reformer reappears, do not think that the entire world would be put aright in a day! Rather, it is by hard work and sacrifices that the oppressors would be exterminated. If you think, as some misguided laymen do, that for reappearance of that graceful Imam, the world must be entirely overwhelmed with cruelty and injustice so that the Imam should reappear sooner, then we should seek refuge in God

Q. My advice to all Muslims and oppressed peoples of the world is that you should not sit and wait till your own authorities or rulers, or some foreign powers make a gift of freedom and independence to you. During the last century, we have observed the infiltration of the world's major powers into all Islamic countries and smaller lands. Reliable history has related this for us. None of the rulers of any of these countries have been concerned with freedom, independence and welfare of his nation. Rather the majority of such rulers have been cruel oppressors who tried to strangulate their own people. Whatever good they did was to benefit themselves or some special group. Such rulers promoted the welfare of the already well-to-do classes but never did a thing to benefit the deprived groups and slum-dwellers. These last groups were deprived even of their daily bread. The miserable and deprived groups were taken into the service of the profligate pleasure-seeking or they were made puppets of big powers, doing their best to make their countries more and more dependent on foreign powers. The rulers of such countries, who were only nominal, secured the interests of their Eastern or Western masters, turned their countries into markets for the consumption of the manufactured products of their overlords and kept their own homelands in an undeveloped condition. They are doing so even now.

O, you deprived people of the world! O, you Muslims and Muslim countries of the world! Rise up and fight for your rights! Do not be afraid of the propaganda operations of the superpowers and their mercenaries. Drive out from your lands your wicked rulers who hand over your earnings to your enemies and the enemies of Islam. You, yourselves and the dedicated public servants should take charge of the affairs of your country. Gather, all of you, under the proud banner of Islam and fight the enemies of Islam and of the deprived peoples of the world. Advance toward an Islamic sovereign government with so many free and independent republics. If you realize this, the arrogant powers would retreat to their own places. All deprived people would come to inherit the earth and attain guardianship over it. Looking forward to the day when Allah's promise shall be fulfilled!

R. At the conclusion of this testament once more I say to the honorable Iranian nation that in this world the vastness of one's pains, sufferings, devotion, deprivations and sacrifices is commensurate with the vastness of one's cause and its value and station. You, noble nation, have risen and given your lives and wealth for the noblest, most sublime and most valuable cause. This cause has been put forth since time began. No such cause would be ever presented again. This cause is the 'school of divinity' in its broad sense. It is the idea of Monotheism in its lofty dimensions whose ultimate and creative foundation lies throughout the expanse of the world of being. It unfolds at the levels and degrees of Occultation and Presence as made fully manifest in the school of Muhammad the Prophet (*s*). For its realization, the Prophets and the Divine Guardians (*s*) worked hard. Absolute perfection and utmost glory and beauty cannot be attained except by the Supreme Divinity Who has exalted the earthly man above the heavenly beings. That which accrues to the earthly man from progression in His path does not accrue to any other being whether perceptible by the eye or veiled.

O you, the struggling nation! Move under an emblem and banner waving everywhere in the moral and material world! Whether you are aware of it or not, you are treading a path that was traversed by all Prophets. It is the only path to happiness and bliss! This is the incentive of the prophets in accepting and embracing martyrdom. This is what makes martyrdom sweeter than honey to them. Your youth have experienced this at the battlegrounds. It has made them live in ecstasy ever since. It is reflected in the soul and conduct of the brothers, sisters and families of the martyrs. We should truly say: *"We wish we were with you (the martyrs), perhaps we, too, could be blessed and receive salvation."* May they enjoy the breeze that delights the heart and that exhilarating manifest.

We should know that a fragment of that manifestation is displayed in the hot and agricultural cultivated fields, in enervating factories and workshops and in industrial centers of research, development, and inventions. It was partially reflected among the nation on the whole; in the bazaar, in the streets and in rural areas. Only a portion of it was displayed among all who those serve Islam and the Islamic Republic, working toward progress and self-sufficiency.

As long as this spirit of cooperation and dedication prevails in the society, our country shall, by Allah's will, be immune to worldly woes. Thank God that the theological centers, the universities and the younger generation in educational institutions have all been blessed with the Divine spirit. They have control over all these agencies, which are safe from encroachment by the saboteurs and perverts.

My advice to all is to advance towards self-awareness, self-sufficiency and independence with the remembrance of Almighty God. Without any doubt, His Hand is with you if you are with Him and continue with this spirit of cooperation for the advancement of the Islamic country.

I pray that what I observe in the noble nation as alertness, intelligence, commitment, devotion, spirit of resistance and courage being employed in the path of Allah, shall, by His Grace, be transmitted to the successive future generations with increased momentum.

With a peaceful mind, a certain heart, a happy soul, and a conscience hopeful for Allah's mercy, I take my leave of all brothers and sisters to journey to the eternal abode. I need your prayers and beg for Almighty God's pardon and forgiveness for my inadequacies.

I hope, the nation, too, will forgive my shortcomings and failings, move ahead with power and determination and know that the departure of a single servant shall not leave a scratch on the steel shield that is the nation. Worthier servants of greater stature are in service and Allah preserves the nation and the oppressed people of the world.

May God's peace be upon you and His righteous servants.

Ruhullah al-Musawi al-Khomeini
February 15, 1983 [Bahman 26, 1361 AHS / Jamadi-al-Awwal 1, 1403 AH]

In His Most Exalted Name

My son Ahmad will read this will and testament to the people after my death. If he has any excuses for not doing so, the President of the Islamic Republic or the Speaker of the Islamic Consultative Assembly or the President of the State Supreme Court shall kindly accept the task, if they too, are excused, let one of the religious authorities of the Guardian Council accept the trouble.

Ruhullah al-Musawi al-Khomeini

In His Most Exalted Name

I would like to add at the end of this will and testament with its prologue the following points:

1. While still here with you, I would like to declare that certain false statements have already been imputed to me; this state of affairs might may increase after I am gone. Therefore, I hereby declare that nothing ascribed to me has my confirmation unless it is in my handwriting, has my signature or is my voice confirmed by experts, or what I have said on the television of the Islamic Republic.

2. Some individuals have claimed, even while I am alive, that they have been writing my statements. This is hereby denied. All such statements have been prepared and written by myself only.

3. Apparently some claim to have arranged my visit to Paris, France. This is a lie. After I was turned back from Kuwait, I chose Paris in consultation with Ahmad for it was probable that Islamic states would decline admission as they were under the Shah's influence but Paris was not.

4. In the course of the movement and the Revolution, I spoke favorably of certain individuals who had pretentions to Islam but I later realized their deception. My favorable comments were made at a time when they pretended to be committed to the Islamic Republic. Such matters should not be taken advantage of. The criterion for everyone is his current conduct.

Ruhullah al-Musawi al-Khomeini

Endnotes:

The following are explanations of terms and phases in the testament of Imam Khomeini written by the Institute for Compilation and Publication of Imam Khomeini's Works:

1. The Messenger of God (s) said: I am leaving among you two weighty things [*thaqalayn*]: the Book of God and my progeny (i.e. Imam Ali and the other purified Imams (*a*) as explained in other traditions). These two will never separate from each other until they meet me at the Pond of Kawthar (i.e. until the Day of Judgment).

2. This is the vanguard of the politico-religious testament, which that eminent *qiblah* of the people of the heart has began his immortal testament with sentences containing the loftiest subjects of Islamic knowledge.

3. Imam Khomeini has divided the world of creation into three realms as follows: (1) material, (2) celestial and (3) intellectual.

4. The Messenger of God (s) said: "Verily, the Quran has exterior and interior (forms) and its interior has seven interiors. See *Tafsir as-Safi*, Preliminary 8.
   Imam al-Baqir (*a*) said: "Except for the successors of the Prophet, nobody can claim to know the interior and exterior of the entire Quran." See *al-Usul Min al-Kafi*, vol. 1, p. 228.
   The Commander of the Faithful (*a*) said: "Verily, the affairs of us, Household of the Prophet, is difficult and arduous. Except the Archangel, commissioned prophet or noble faithful whose heart has been endowed with faith by God, nobody can acquire such knowledge or comprehend it." See *Basair ad-Darajat*, p. 27.
   Abu Abdullah al-Husayn (*a*) said: "Verily, the affairs of us, Household of the Prophet, is a secret within a secret, a hidden secret, a secret that has no benefit except another secret, a secret over another secret and secret hidden behind another secret." See *Basair ad-Darajat*, p. 28.

5. By "greater weighty thing" is meant the Book of God, the Quran while "great weighty thing" signifies the Household of the Prophet (*a*). Since the Quran is greater than all things including the Household of the Prophet, it is the greater absolute.

The Noble Prophet (s) is reported to have observed:
"O people, verily I am leaving among you two weighty things [*thaqalayn*]. If you firmly adhere to them, you will never go astray after me. One is greater than the other: the Book of God which may be likened to a rope extended from Heaven to earth and my progeny. Be aware that these two will never separate from each other until they meet me at the Pond of *Kawthar*." See *Bihar al-Anwar*, "*kitab al-Imamah*," vol. 23, p. 117.

6. It refers to the collective return of the creatures and physical realms to their celestial essences on the Day of Resurrection and the Hereafter. In other words, it is the return of multiplicity in the world of being to a unity from which it has emanated. It is the same station of the union of multiplicity with unity.

7. This is a term related to *hadith* and principles of jurisprudence. IIt is a report transmitted by a congregation such that it is an important knowledge, i.e. a common knowledge and it is impossible all have combined in fabricating it. In short, one of the ways of acquiring common knowledge is the *mutawatir* report or news. Most of our information and knowledge in relation to historical affairs is through this way. Thus, sometimes a number of people transmit a report uniformly, or it is similar in thought and not in wordings. It is impossible that all have combined (in fabricating it); therefore, what is important will be the certainty. See *Farhang-e Ulum Doktor Sajjadi beh Naql az Maalim*, p. 101; *Talwih-e Taftazani*, p. 429.

8. *Sahih Sittah* ["Six Authentic Collections"] are the following in chronological order: (1) *Sahih al-Bukhari* or *Al-Jami as-Sahih* by Abu Abdillah Muhammad ibn Ismail al-Bukhari (d. 256 AH); (2) *Sahih Muslim* by Abul-Husayn Muslim ibn Hajjaj Qashiri Nayshaburi (d. 261 AH); (3) *Sunan ibn Majah* by Muhammad ibn Yazid ibn Majah al-Qazwini (d. 273 AH); (4) *Sunan ibn Dawud* by Sulayman ibn Ashath ibn Ishaq as-Sajistani (d. 275 AH); (5) *Jami at-Tirmidhi* or *Sunan at-Tirmidhi* by Abu Isa Muhammad ibn Isa ibn as-Sawrah (d. 279 AH); and (6) *Sunan Nisai* (called Mujtaba) by Abu Abdur-Rahman Ahmad ibn Shuayb (d. 303 AH).

The abovementioned books, with the addition of *al-Muwatta* and *Musnad ibn Hanbal* by Ahmad ibn Hanbal (d. 241 AH), constitute the primary *hadith* collections of narrations by Sunni people.

9. For information on the abundant references and proof of this noble *hadith*'s *tawatur* [uninterruptedly transmitted], one can refer to the valuable book, *Aqabat al-Anwar*, written by the great *mujahid* (religious authority), Allamah Mir Hamid Husayn Hindi (d. 1306 AH) whose six volumes are allotted for the sources and commentary of this *hadith* through the Sunni *ulama*.

In this precious work, the revered scholar has cited 40 books for this *Hadith ath-Thaqalayn* [*Hadith* on the Two Weighty Things] from the Sunni sources. He has also pointed out that the Sunni transmitters of this noble *hadith* in chronological order have been 16 persons during the 2nd century, 33 during the 3rd century, 21 during the 4th century, 13 each during the 5th and 6th century, 16 during the 7th century, 17 during the 8th century, 5 during the 9th century, 18 during the 10th century, 10 during the 11th century, 13 during the 12th century and 11 persons during the 13th century. They are among the great Sunni figures.

In *Ghayah al-Maram*, section 28 about the *Hadith ath-Thaqalayn* Allamah Sayyid Hashim Behrani cited 82 ways for this *hadith* through the Shiah *hadith*s and *hadith* scholars.

In this manner, this noble *hadith* has been transmitted with 268 sources from both Sunnis and Shiah's, and thus there is no doubt concerning its *tawatur*.

10. Based on the noble *ayah*, *"And Adam knew all their names"* (*Surah al-Baqarah* 2:31), Hadrat Adam (*a*) through the divine teachings became the one knowledgeable of the names and thus deserving of being the vicegerency of God on earth.

By "the son of the knowledge of names" Imam Khomeini is referring to the human beings who are all sons of Hadrat Adam.

11. *Nahj al-Balaghah* (Peak of Eloquence) is a collection of sermons, wise sayings and letters of the Commander of the Faithful, Imam Ali ibn Abi Talib (*a*) compiled by Sharif ar-Radi Muhammad ibn al-Husayn (d. 406 AH/1016). Contents of the book concern the three essential topics of God, man and the universe, also including comments on scientific, literary, social, ethical, and political issues. Not only to the words of the Glorious Quran and of the Holy Prophet (*s*), but also no other words of man can equate it in eloquence. So far, more than 101 exegeses have been written on the *Nahj al-Balaghah*, indicating the importance of this treatise for scholars and learned men of research. For more information, visit: http://www.al-islam.org/nahjul.

12. "Ascending Quran" is referring to the supplications recited by the Infallibles (*a*).

13. The accomplished scholar, Ali ibn Tawus, narrates this prayer in "the practices of the month of Shaban" from Husayn ibn Muhammad ibn Khaluyah. He writes that the Commander of the Faithful and his children (*a*) always recite this prayer during the month of Shaban. See *Iqbal al-Amal*, p. 685; *Mafatih al-Jinan*, "practices on the Day of Arafah."

14. The valuable *Dua Arafah* [Supplication in Arafah] is a litany that Hadrat Aba Abdillah al-Husayn (*a*) recited in the afternoon of the Day of Arafah in open sky at the plain of Arafah while shedding with rain-like tears. See *Iqbal al-Amal*, "practices on the Day of Arafah," p. 339; *Zad al-Imad*, p. 265; *Mafatih al-Jinan*, "practices on the Day of Arafah."

This supplication is expressive of the loving secret and need of the Chief of the Freemen and the Doyen of the Martyrs with his Beloved and Object of Worship, the Sole Creator, and comprising extremely high and profound concepts.

15. Imam as-Sadiq (*a*) said: "Fatimah remained alive for 75 days after the demise of the Noble Prophet (*s*). During this span of time, she lamented for the passing away of her father. On account of this, Jibril (Gabriel) regularly visited her and wished for her health that was deteriorating due to lamenting for her father. The angel was her consoler. At times, he would talk about the status and station of her revered father, while at other times he would inform her of the events to befall her progeny after her. The Commander of the Faithful (*a*) would wrote all the things that Jibril said to her, being known as *Mushaf Fatimah*. See *Al-Usul min al-Kafi*, vol. 1, p. 241. In another *hadith* in the book, *Al-Kafi*, the Commander of the Faithful (*a*) is reported to have said: "In this *Mushaf* not only lawful and unlawful things but also knowledge of what has happened and would happen were discussed."

16. *Baqir al-Ulum*: The blessed name of His Holiness is Muhammad and his famous title Baqir. The title was given to him by the Messenger (*s*) according to a certain narration. His famous epithet is Abu Jafar and his age was 57.

Among the Imams (*a*) Imam al-Baqir has two merits. First, his paternal grandfather is Imam al-Husayn (*a*) while his maternal grandfather is Imam al-Hasan (*a*). In view of this, he is rightfully called, "the Alawi (related to

Imam Ali) among the Alawis, the Fatimi (related to Lady Fatimah) among the Fatimis, and the Hashimi (related to the Hashimite clan) among the Hashimis".

His other merit is that he was the founder of Shiah cultural revolution. Though the spread of Shiah learning was done by Imam as-Sadiq (*a*), it was founded by Imam al-Baqir. During the period of Imam al-Baqir (*a*) the Umayyad dynasty was in decline and the people abhorred it. Owing to the existence of persons such as Umar ibn Abdul-Aziz, which apart from the fact that it was greatly beneficial for the Shiah, fatally harmful for the Umayyads, brought into being serious discord in the Muslim lands, and every one in the corner was rising up, the caliphs were easily replacing one another such that during the Imamate of Imam al-Baqir for 19 years, five caliphs came to the office of the caliphate: Walid ibn Abdul-Malik, Sulayman ibn Abdul-Malik, Umar ibn Abdul-Aziz, Yazid ibn Abdul-Malik, and Hisham ibn Abdul-Malik. Thus, being relieved from the oppression of the Umayyads was a golden opportunity for him to commence the intellectual revolution. He gathered great men from among Sunnis and Shiahs around him and propagated the truth of Islam, the favors of Islam and finally the teachings of Islam. On this account, the Noble Messenger (*s*) has given him the title, "Al-Baqir". The author of *Lisan al-Arab* says: "Imam al-Baqir is addressed with this title because he is the Cleaver of Knowledge. He understood the foundation of the Islamic sciences, comprehended their branches, propagated them and spread root means propagated one.

Both Sunnis and Shiahs narrate that the Noble Messenger (*s*) has said to Jabir ibn Abdillah al-Ansari: "O Jabir! You will remain alive and meet a man from the progeny of al-Husayn. His name is Muhammad who will cleave the knowledge of the prophets. When you meet him, extend my greetings to him."

17. Zionism is an extremist thinking of the fanatic Jewish capitalists, which came into being in Europe during the latter part of the past century and has now become the official ideology of the Quds-occupier regime. The name is derived from "Zion", a mountain near Jerusalem.

Zionism is based on racial discrimination and considers the Jewish people to have a special status in the world. Believing to bee the Chosen People of God, they have a special mission. On the basis of this thinking, in 1897 a society named International Zionist Congress came into being whose objective is to transfer the Jews around the world to Palestine. Now, this Congress has an enormous financial power equal to that of the largest monopolist companies of the world. Its center is located in the United States of America, controlling the activities of the Zionist societies in more than 16 countries in the world. At present, nearly 18 Zionist organizations are active in the world. Similarly, in the US there are 281 national Jewish organizations, 251 Jewish local federations as well as different kinds of advisory societies, funds and others. The US government is one of the principal supporters of the International Zionism which has intelligence and espionage centers in most countries of the world, having contacts with the Mossad and CIA.

The most important and effective weapon of the International Zionism is utilization of the mass media the world over. A total of 1,036 newspapers and magazines are at the disposal of the International Zionism, the most famous of which being the New York Times.

18. From the beginning, the followers of Zionism have been striving for the realization of a fundamental and main aim: establishment of a Jewish state and global government under the Jewish dominance under the name of, Greater Israel in Palestine. Based on this, after establishing the State of Israel in 1948, the Zionists have been determined to create the Greater Israel. In justifying this policy of theirs, they considered this policy to be in conformity with the teachings of the Torah.

The map of Greater Israel encompass many Muslim countries or parts of them. The said map exists in the research report of Benjamin Marzar (?), which was published under the supervision of the Israeli government. In the said map, they have defined the territory of Israel as extending from the Nile to the Euphrates Rivers, and Israel as encompassing the entire Persian Gulf, Northern Iraq, Muscat, Oman, Najaf, Turkey, Syria, South Lebanon, East Palestine, West Jordan, part of Egypt and South Sudan. In addition, the map of the Greater Israel, which can be the next phase after realizing the Great Israel design, also includes Kurdistan, southeastern region of Iran, southwestern Afghanistan and part of northwestern Pakistan.

19. Husayn Bin Talal was born on November 4, 1935 in Amman, Jordan. He spent his childhood in the British kindergarten in Amman. Then, he studied at the Victoria Academy of Alexandria, Egypt, and continued his studies at Harrow School in London, England. In 1951, his grandfather, Abdullah, was killed by a young revolutionary Palestinian. His influence in his family and the policy of Britain demanded that the monarchy should remain in this

family; hence, with the British aid, Talal, the father of Hussayn, was crowned King, and Husayn, the Crown Prince.

Few months after the coming to power of Talal on August 11, 1952, the rubberstamp parliament of Jordan declared him unfit to rule and designated King Husayn in his stead. After this succession, King Husayn became the bridge of the British and on May 2, 1953, he returned to Jordan and took control of the government. Throughout his rule, he had always enjoyed the British support.

Following the British withdrawal from East Suez Canal and the gradual replacement of America in the region, he earned the American support. The policies of King Husayn's government in the Middle East have been always towing the lines of the American and British policies. In 1967 when the Arab-Israeli War erupted, the Zionists were able to occupy the West Bank of the Jordan River and annex it to Israel thanks to betrayal of King Husayn. As a result, 400,000 Palestinians were displaced and driven to Jordan. King Jordan not only did not make any step in fighting for the legitimate rights of the Palestinians but also left forever an ignominious stain on the government of Jordan through the September 1970 tragedy, known as Black September, by killing the oppressed people and displaced Palestinians in the Jordanian soil.

20. King Hasan of Morocco, the son of Sultan Muhammad V, was born in 1929. He has studied in France. After passing away of his father, he ascended the throne under the name, Sultan Hasan II. With coming to power of King Hasan II, France-Morocco relations were extended as it was expected. Morocco was subjected to cultural onslaught by the West more than in the past. Morocco also enjoyed the support of France in cultural, economic and political sectors.

It is said that Anwar Sadat, the treacherous president of Egypt, he was associated, was introduced to the Zionists by King Hasan because he had longtime relations with them and because the annual conference of Jews is held in Morocco. Perhaps it is the only Arab country wherein the Zionists have officially freedom of action to such an extent that in 1991 King Hasan appointed a Jew named Andara Azuli as his supreme adviser (?).

21. Husni Mubarak was born in the province of al-Manufiyyah, Egypt in 1928. In 1947, he entered the Military Sciences University, taking aeronautics training courses there. Later, he went to the Soviet Union for completion of his training.

He became the Commander-in-Chief of the Air Force in 1972. During the Arab-Israeli War in October 1973, Mubarak was the Air Force Commander of Egypt.

He was one of closest allies of Anwar Sadat, the architect of the disgraceful Camp David Accord, attending his important meetings.

He married a British woman named Susanne and has two sons named Ala and Jamal.

After the assassination of Sadat at the hands of the revolutionary colonel, Martyr Khalid Islambuli in 1981, Mubarak took the helms of affairs of Egypt. He announced that he would pursue all the policies of Sadat in domestic and foreign areas. In an interview by the American ABS TV channel in 1982, he said: "Our gates are open to the Arab friends but not at the expense of severing our relations with Israel. We can play a good role in eliminating any kind of confusion that would come into being anytime between Arabs and Israel."

22. "Titles"—that is, actions and essences—on which there is a religious ruling are in two conditions:

a) The first condition: the "title"—reconsideration of whatever condition and attribute for which has a ruling—is called primary ruling or law.

b) The second condition: the "title"—in case new condition and attribute must be formulated for which such as state of compulsion, unwillingness, fault, loss, corruption, etc.—is called secondary ruling or law. For example, eating the flesh of corpse, as a "primary title", is unlawful, but if the person is in a state of compulsion or necessity, he is permitted in doing so. See Ayatullah Ali Mishkini, *Istilahat al-Usul [Terminologies on the Principles of Jurisprudence]*, p. 124.

23. National tendencies are not absolutely abominable and wrong. Instead, that which is abominable is that kind of nationalist tendency that trigger separation of races and nations from one another and creates discrimination and division. Naturally, if "nationalism" is confined to a simple feeling of love toward the land, homeland and nation, it does not become a sort of idol to be worshipped, and does not sacrifice all the divine truths before its altar, it will not be blameworthy. However, if this feeling is supposed to replace the humane and Islamic truths and values, to be excessively given attention and consideration as a lofty value, and to emerge as a school and ideology, it will not bring anything except misguidance, polytheism and corruption. Islam is strongly opposed to such tendency.

Martyr Murtada Mutahhari (may God be pleased with him), in this regard, writes: "Nationalism is rationally condemnable when it assumes negative aspect for itself; that is, when it separates individuals from one another under the name of different nations, bring about hostile relations among them and disregards the true rights of others..." See Murtada Mutahhari, *Islam and Iran: A Historical Study of Mutual Services*, http://www.al-islam.org/al-tawhid/iran/mutual.htm.

Imam Khomeini has repeatedly pointed out the menace of nationalism and nationalist tendencies, describing them as factor responsible for discord and separation among nations and hindrance for the advancement of Islam: "Through the hands of the corrupt governments, these racisms and factionalisms among Muslims have developed; placing the Arabs against the Persians, the Persians against the Arabs and the Turks, and the Turks against the others, and all races against one another. The reason why I repeatedly point out that this nationalism is the source of misfortune for Muslims is that this nationalism places the nation of Iran against the other Muslim nations, the Iraqi nation against the others, and a certain nation against another nation. These are plots woven by imperialists in order for the Muslims not to be united..."

24. *Hudud* is the plural form of *hadd* and literally means hindrance, gap between two things and the endpoint of anything. *Tazirat* is the plural form of *tazir* and literally means to reproach and to blame. While technically describing *hadd* and *tazir*, Muhaqqiq Hilli said to the effect:

Hadd: whenever the punishment for a crime is specified by the canon, it is called *hadd*; for example, punishments for stealing, murder, etc.

Tazir: whenever the punishment for a crime is not specified by the canon, it is called *tazir* and its limit is entirely determined by the judge and competent jurist. See Shahid ath-Thani, *Sharh al-Lumah*, "kitab al-hudud wat-tazirat"; Muhaqqiq al-Hilli, *Kitab al-Hudud wat-Tazirat*.

25. Surah at-Tawbah 9:38-39: *"O ye who believe! What aileth you that when it is said unto you: Go forth in the way of Allah, ye are bowed down to the ground with heaviness. Take ye pleasure in the life of the world rather than in the Hereafter? The comfort of the life of the world is but little in the Hereafter. If ye go not forth He will afflict you with a painful doom, and will choose instead of you a folk other then you Ye cannot harm Him at all. Allah is Able to do all things."*

26. "And verily, at the time of the Messegner of God (s), they told lies to him to such an extent that he stood up to deliver a sermon, saying: "Whoever intentionally and knowingly tells a lie on me, his abode will be in the fire of hell." Fayd al-Islam, *Nahj al-Balaghah* Sermon 201.

27. *Surah Muhammad* 47:7: *"O ye who believe! If ye help Allah, He will help you and will make your foothold firm."*

28. The communist organization, *Cherik-ha-ye Fadai-ye Khalq* [Guerillas Devoted to the People], was organized in 1349 AHS by the youth who were dissatisfied with the policies of the Tudeh Party that was dependent on the Soviet Union. They chose the Alborz mountain ranges, Siyahkol jungle in particular, as their base for operation and incited the villagers of the region to rise up against the regime. With the effort of the Shah's regime, this organization suffered a painful defeat in early 1354 AHS. In Ordibehesht and Khordad 1355 AHS it disintegrated. After this defeat, nothing was seen from them except a few cases of assassination and clash with the police forces in operation. With the beginning of the Islamic Revolution and the creation of a favorable atmosphere, the organization reorganized itself and intensified its resistance against the Army and revolutionary forces from early 1357 AHS. Of course, in comparison with the roaring wave of the people who, under the guidance of their leader and savior, His Eminence Imam Khomeini, had made tyranny tremble, this intensity of resistance was inconsiderable. With the victory of the Islamic Revolution, this organization stuck on its imported principles and policy notwithstanding its lack of popular base. Thus, in tandem with the World Arrogance, it engaged in opposing the Islamic Revolution and assassinating common people and religious forces. With the discovery of their large bases and team houses, the organization was divided into the majority and minority branches. The majority, in consonance with the Tudeh Party, identified the principle on political negotiation to earn reputation while the minority adhered to armed struggle and selected Kurdistan for continuation of its operation. Finally, through the effort of the self-sacrificing Muslim people of Kurdistan and forces loyal to the revolution, they left the region and escaped abroad.

29. *Tudeh* (Masses) Party was formed in 1320 AHS on the remnants of the *Idalat* (Justice) Party, which was created in 1299 AHS after the entry of the Red Army to Rasht. In line with the policy pursued by Qawwam as-Saltanah of emptying Iran, three communist ministers entered the cabinet. With the

exit of the Russian forces, the defeat of the Democrat Party of Azerbaijan and the split occurred within the party in 1326 AHS, some members experimented the party's independence from the Soviet Union. Following an attempt on the life of the Shah in Bahman 1327 AHS for which a Tudeh assailant was identified, martial law was declared, members of the party apprehended and the party considered illegitimate and dissolved. By announcing Marxism-Leninism as the party's platform in 1328 AHS, it completely revealed its policy. With the beginning of nationalization of the oil industry, Tudeh Party assumed two factions—that of Kiyanuri and Qasimi. Later, by keeping silent in face of Mordad 28, 1332 AHS coup and behind-the-scene activities, it played a pivotal role in the fall of Musaddiq. With the arrest of officers of military and other networks of the party by the Shah's regime in Mordad 1333 AHS, so many expressed disgust for their party's backgrounds and collaborated with the Shah's regime and its security organization. In the party's congress itself in early 1950s, the party praised the regime and discouraged resistance. From 1350 to 1356 AHS when the clergy started the struggle with new methods, the Party reorganized itself. After the victory of the Islamic Revolution, it held its 16th party congress in Tehran and announced its support for the Islamic Republic. The party's objective after the Islamic Revolution was to incite dissension among the revolutionary forces in graduation and infiltrate the economic and cultural posts of the country. Finally, with the arrest of the principal leaders and cadres of the Tudeh Party, a wave of confessions commenced. With the lengthy and extensive confessions of figures such as Kiyanuri and Tabari on espionage and endeavor to destroy the Islamic system, the true nature of this party became known to everyone and its 42 years of treacherous existence in Iran came to an end.

30. Iosif Vissarionovich Dzhugashvili, known as Jospeh Stalin, was born on December 21, 1879 in Georgia. He was introduced to Marxism at the age of 15. From then on, he engaged in political activities. Because of these activities, he was apprehended and imprisoned for many times.

In 1907, at the Conference of Social Democrats of Russia in London, Lenin bestowed him the title, "Stalin", meaning "man of steel" in Russian.

The 341,000 ruble robbery of Tbilisi Bank on June 26, 1906, the then biggest robbery, made him a famous hero among the communists.

In 1912, the Bolshevik Party was formally organized. At the suggestion of Lenin, Stalin became member of its Central Committee. Later, he published the newspaper, *Zuzda* (?) and then *Pravda* [Truth]. Following the victory of the October Revolution, at Lenin's behest, he became a member of the new government's Soviet (Council) of People's Commissars (Russian acronym, Sovnarkom), heading the Commissariat for Nationality Affairs. He was elected Secretary General of the Communist Party in 1922 and took control of its organization.

Lenin died on January 21, 1924. His testament, which had an expression of his discontentment with Stalin, along with his anti-Stalin articles strong, was handed over by his widow to Kamenev, who in turn handed it over to the Political Bureau of the Party. This affair generated the anger of Stalin and became the prelude to his subsequent bloody purge. With the seven-hour speech of Stalin at the 15th Congress of the Party in December 1927, the plan to accelerate the advancement of communism was approved. The collectivization of agriculture was one of its manifestations, leading to the murder of 10 million kulaks or affluent farmers during the Tsarist period. Stalin then pursued his bloody purges until 1939; only in 1935, some 536,500 people were killed. With the outbreak of the World War II and the occupation of Poland, Lithuania, Latvia, and Estonia, Stalin advanced the Soviet Union into a global power.

Finally, this infamous dictator of history died in a suspicious manner on March 5, 1953 and his 30-year rule of strangulation, terror and murder came to an end.

31. Amol Incident happened on Khordad 30, 1360 AHS following the announcement of armed resistance of the oppositionists against the nascent Islamic system. By evaluating the geographical conditions, the Union of Communists in Iran, consisting of Marxist-Leninist leftists, identified the jungles of Amol as appropriate for guerilla operations and stationed there. The idle imagination of the union was that owing to the social condition of Amol region and the population fabric of the surrounding villages, in case of attack on the city, the sporadic resistance of the revolutionary forces would be swiftly suppressed. In the second phase after cutting off the communication lines and consolidating the opposition forces inside the city, the other regions of Mazandaran would be occupied by the union. Thereafter, the whole people, in chain reaction throughout Iran, would rise up and the Islamic Republic would fall.

Their assault began on the night of Bahman 6. They were divided into two groups. The first group entered the city, patrolling around and assassinating anyone whom they identified as so-called "*Hizbullahi*". They then attacked the Islamic Revolutionary Committee of the city. The people of Amol, who had come to the streets due to the gunfire and become aware of the happenings, became ready for confrontation. On the following morning, the epic struggle of the people commenced. Through entrenchment in the city and confronting the forces of the union, the people of Amol shattered their formation. As a result, the forces of the union, which had not taken the people's faith and resistance into consideration, were divided into smaller groups. However, because of the intensity of the people's resistance, their communication with one another was cut and until the sunset they were routed. In this happening 34 communists killed, some wounded and 30 taken captives, while 40 of the noble people of Amol were martyred.

32. The term, "American communist" is used in relation to the operation of some leftist parties in different countries of the world, especially in Muslim countries. Though apparently believing in the principles and fundamentals of communism, these parties are toeing the line of the Western policies in their stances and conducts.

Like so many communist parties in Iran, such as Paykar, Kumeleh and Democrat, which had always tried to topple down the Islamic Republic of Iran in tandem with the policies of the CIA, were receiving financial aids from the World Arrogance. In a more in-depth study, it can be said that, in general, the communists' confrontation with the Islamist movement in Muslim countries, particularly in Iran, irrespective of the slogans and kind of relations and dependency of the communist parties to the member countries of the communist bloc in the past, has always been in line with the interests and in consonance with the hostile policies of America and the West against the Islamic Revolution.

33. This party was founded in 1322 AHS by Qadi Muhammad through the sponsorship and encouragement of the ex-Soviet Union.

In Bahman 1324 AHS, Qadi Muhammad, as the Secretary General of the Party, established a government in Mahabad in line with the Soviet policies and the disintegration of Iran, but after the treaty between Iran and the ex-Soviet Union, Qadi Muhammad along with his brother, Sayf Qadi, and about forty to fifty members of the Party were executed.

In 1338 AHS, attempts were made to revive the party, but ended in failure.

With the passage of time and the victory of the Islamic Revolution in Iran, this Party again started activity. By making use of the party's background and exploiting the weakness of the provisional government and with some treacheries, its new leaders succeeded in consolidating their position in some parts of Kurdistan by occupying a number of military camps and looting the arms. Ideologically, though leaning on Marxism, the Democrat Party did not believe in the validity of class struggle. On account of this, local feudal lords and khans were occupying special positions within the Party and its cadre of leaders.

After the Islamic Revolution, the leadership of the Party was shouldered by Abdur-Rahman Qasimlu. In 1338 AHS, by giving commitment to the Shah's SAVAK, he left Iran. He resided in the Soviet Union, Iraq, Eastern Europe and France for15 years. In France, he engaged in activity in as-Sanah ash-Sharqiyyah, one of whose functions is to teach and train spies in Eastern countries. During his stay in the Soviet Union, he was busy broadcasting in the Persian radio service. In Iraq, he had also an important government position. His family is among the notable feudal chiefs of the region.

On Monday, Tir 22, 1368 AHS, Qasimlu was assassinated in Vienna, Austria. Under the guise of "autonomy", the Democrat Party's strategy was the secession of Kurdistan from the Islamic Republic of Iran. Like other parties in the region, with continued schisms within its structure, this Party became aimless and went astray. Its existence largely depended on the Baath Party and its Western patrons.

Based on the documents obtained from the American den of espionage in Iran, the American government has made the maximum use of the Democrat Party in exerting pressure on the nascent Islamic system. Continuous creation of disorder in the region and complete support for the Democrat Party and other belligerent groups in Kurdistan were part of the CIA programs.

34. According to the claim of this party, 1348 AHS is its founding year but its lack of any form of activity until 1357 AHS and absence of sufficient evidence make this claim seems doubtful. In 1357 AHS, following the murder of a certain Muhammad Hasan Karimi whom the party considered one of its members, the party proclaimed existence. Thereafter, in a bid to acquire funds and mobilizations acceptable to the people, it exploited the suburbs by chanting the slogans of defending the peasants against the feudal lords of Kermanu. In view of the particular background, psyche and culture prevalent in the region, their common deceitful slogans proved effective to a considerable extent and brought into being an anti-government atmosphere in the region. Along with this, through the arms they plundered from the military headquarters of the region and the sorts of assistance they were receiving from the Baathist regime, they entered into an armed confrontation with the Islamic Republic. Ideologically, this Party has taken inspiration

from the viewpoints of Mao. After the expansion of the military mobilization of the Islamic Republic, the organization set up by the said group was shattered and their remains sought refuge in the town of Bukan.

Considering its affiliation to the World Arrogance and the aids of the Baathist regime to it, Kumeleh Party took stance in tune with the propaganda blows against the Islamic Republic of Iran in the imposed war and announced Iran as responsible for the war. Throughout the war, members of the Kumeleh, like other communist and hypocrite parties, acted as the fifth column of the enemy and worked as mercenaries of the Iraqi government.

In terms of morality, by proposing ideas such as "free love" and others, this party showed the moral corruptions of its interior.

Anyhow, the current transformations in the Kurdistan region and the consolidation of power of the central government in the region led to the total isolation and extermination of the Kumeleh Party. The Iranian people recognize this party alongside the hypocrites (MKO) and as one of the most detested parties committing treason to the nation and the Islamic Revolution.

35. Sayyid Hasan Mudarris (1859-1938) was one of the greatest religious and political figures in the recent history of Iran. He received his elementary education in Isfahan. He then traveled to Iraq to visit the holy shrines of the imams buried in Najaf, Karbala and Kazimayn. There, he received further education under guidance of such scholars as Mulla Muhammad Kazim Khorasani. After graduation to the level of *ijtihad,* he returned to Isfahan and began teaching Islamic jurisprudence (*fiqh*) and its principles (*usul*). In 1909, at the time of the Second National Assembly, he entered parliament. He was chosen by the *maraji at-taqlid* and the *ulama* of Najaf as one of the five *mujtahid*s who were to oversee the law-making procedures. At the time of the Third National Assembly, he was chosen as a member of parliament. When Rida Khan carried out his coup d'état, Mudarris was arrested and sent into exile, but after being freed he was again chosen by the people to represent them in the parliament. In the Fourth National Assembly, he headed the opposition majority against Rida Khan. At the time of the Fifth and Sixth National Assemblies, he opposed the proposal for establishment of a republic, which Rida Khan was in favor of, to replace the constitutional government. He dissuaded the parliament from approving it. He was resolute in his stand against the stubborn Rida Khan, such that the Shah hired an assassin to kill Mudarris. When he escaped the attempt, Rida Khan sent him first into exile in the remote town of Khaf near the Afghan border and later in Kashmar, where eleven years later in Ramadan 1938, the agents of the Shah

poisoned him. In this way, one of the greatest political and religious personalities of Iran was martyred in the way of Allah. Mudarris possessed outstanding qualities. Even though he was a man of great political and religious influence, he lived a simple life. Imam Khomeini always spoke of him with a great deal of respect. The Leader of the Revolution, on the occasion of the renovation of Mudarris' grave, wrote: "At a time when pens were broken, voices silenced and throats gripped, he never ceased from revealing the truth and abolishing falsehood....this physically weak but spiritually strong scholar was noted for his belief, sincerity and truthfulness and possessing a tongue like the sword of Haydar Karrar (Imam Ali). He stood in front of them, fried out for truth and disclosed the crimes, making life difficult for Rida Khan and blackening his days. Finally, he sacrificed his own pure life in the way of dear Islam and the noble nation and was martyred in exile at the hands of the oppressive Shah's executioner and joined his virtuous forefathers."

36. The Esfand 14, 1359 AHS tragedy was an attempt on the part of the surrogate elements and compromisers to change the direction of the revolution toward a regime acceptable for the West.
On this day, Bani Sadr, the deposed ex-president announce the ceremony commemorating the death anniversary of Dr. Musaddiq at Tehran University with the support of the opposition groups. He delivered an inflammatory speech to mislead the people and isolate the revolutionary forces. The occasion, which started at 3:40 pm, end up in clash between the participants and those opposing it. During the clash, Bani Sadr was inciting the crowd with his inflammatory speech. His special guards along with MKO militias started to harass and beat the dissidents. In this event, many people in and outside of the university were chanting slogans in support of the ideals of the Islamic Revolution. At the order of Bani Sadr, they were assaulted; many of them were injured. The event of Esfand 14 was a turning point, which made clearer and more profound the delineation of the revolutionary forces under the leadership of Imam Khomeini with the deviant lines. This event and acts of Bani Sadr paved the way for his total separation from the people and finally leading to his seeking of refuge in MKO and fall and escape.

37. Following the 1917 October Revolution in Russia and the establishment of communist system there, a very vast part of the world ranging from the Baltic to the Adriatic was under the iron curtain of Marxism. The manifestations of this thought in violence, killing and suppressing the

opposing thoughts were in the most severe possible manner. After the death of Lenin in 1924 and the coming to power of Stalin, the world witnessed the most horrendous killing in the contemporary history. After eliminating his political rivals such as Trotsky, Zinovyev and Kamenev and establishing himself as the supreme leader of the USSR, Stalin implemented his 5-Year Economic Program for the development of the Soviet Union. Abolition of private ownership and collectivization of agricultural system were among the essential policies of this program. In line with this policy, thwarting resistance and opposition were done in the most brutal and inhuman methods. In the forced-labor camps of Gulag (Chief Administration for Corrective Labor Camps) and banishment of accused dissidents in Siberia only, ten million people died. In 1935, under the supervision of Nikolay Yezhov, some 536,500 people were executed. Stalin was afflicted with a disease called, paranoia, whose symptom is megalomania. The policy of killing and repression also persisted during the subsequent periods. During the rule of Brezhnev, the event of Prague Spring and the aggression against Czechoslovakia were accompanied by widespread killings. Most of the crimes of the 70-year rule of the communists in this part of the world were revealed during the coming to power of Gorbachev. Finally, the blaze of the fire of oppression surfaced from the ashes and its vicious flames immediately destroyed the palace of oppression on its dwellers and oppressors.

38. "Sweeter than honey": this expression is used in the *hadith*s in describing the water of the Pond of Kawthar and other favors of the heaven. *Bihar al-Anwar*, vol. 8, pp. 18, 183, 189.

This is also the expression made by Qasim ibn Hasan (*a*) on the night of Ashura in reply to his uncle, Husayn ibn Ali (*a*)… Qasim ibn Hasan (*a*) asked the Imam (*a*): "Am I also among those who will be killed?" The heart of Husayn (*a*) burned for him and asked: "O my son! How is death for you?" He replied: "O uncle! It is sweeter than honey." He (*a*) said: "Yes, I swear to God—may your uncle be your ransom—you are one of the men to be killed with me after being afflicted with great calamity. Haj Mirza Abul-Hasan Sharani's translation of Haj Shaykh Abbas Qummi's *Nafs al-Mahmum*.

39. This is adapted from the last acclivity of the *ziyarat* of Imam Husayn (*a*).

www.ingramcontent.com/pod-product-compliance
Lightning Source LLC
LaVergne TN
LVHW041618070526
838199LV00052B/3198